ANALYZING
FIELD REALITY

JABER GUBRIUM
University of Florida

Qualitative Research Methods,
Volume 8

SAGE PUBLICATIONS
The Publishers of Professional Social Science
Newbury Park   Beverly Hills   London   New Delhi

For information address:

SAGE Publications, Inc.
2111 West Hillcrest Drive
Newbury Park, California 91320

SAGE Publications Inc.
275 South Beverly Drive
Beverly Hills
California 90212

SAGE Publications Ltd.
28 Banner Street
London EC1Y 8QE
England

SAGE PUBLICATIONS India Pvt. Ltd.
M-32 Market
Greater Kailash I
New Delhi 110 048 India

Printed in the United States of America

Library of Congress Cataloging-in-Publication Data

Gubrium, Jaber F.
  Analyzing field reality.

  (Qualitative research methods series ; v. 8)
  Bibliography: p.
  1. Social Structure. 2. Hermeneutics. 3. Ethno-
methodology. I. Title. II. Series: Qualitative
research methods ; v.8.
HM24.G814   1987   305   87-23534
ISBN 0-8039-3095-X
ISBN 0-8039-3096-8 (pbk.)

CONTENTS

For R. Satyanarayana

EDITORS' INTRODUCTION

Many of the assumptions underlying qualitative social research are being questioned. Challenges to conventional thinking found in the works of Harold Garfinkel, Erving Goffman, Anthony Giddens, and French structuralists such as Barthes and Foucault have been especially profound. Such basic theoretic distinctions as macro/micro, structure/process, sign/symbol are being reexamined. Consideration of the role of the observer in the field of observation and the effect of observation on the field now are a part of most field studies. The always somewhat arbitrary lines between data gathering and data analysis, field techniques and role relationships, are also being redrawn. The questions raised are general ones that cross methods and disciplines but are particularly salient in qualitative research. Qualitative work involves the reading of the social world or "text" by interpretation of signs and linking these signs into coherent wholes or structured domains of meaning. Fieldworkers will be engaged in a creative oscillation between data, structure or pattern, and events. Social life has a structure, a flow, and a meaning that is based upon our lived experience. When listening to music, one hears harmony and melody together, and the notes blend into an ongoing song. They exist apart only on paper, and social life, as lived, has an integrated quality that social analysis has as its object.

In this brief book, Gubrium engages the reader in a dialogue about the nature of field data and its interpretation. Although he begins with first-level, or everyday "folk," concepts, he converts them into sociological, or second-order, abstractions by combining structures, data, and events. He summarizes his aim in a sentence: "Analysis proceeds incrementally with the aim of making visible the native practice of clarification, from one domain of experience to another, structure upon structure." It is less about data gathering than about interpretation, and more about structures of meaning than behavior. It views intersubjective reality as a basis for meaning production and reproduction, and challenges the idea that there is a "real world" lying behind the symbols and beliefs we hold. Organization, in this case, a formal organization, is a context or contexts for assigning ████ ████ents, and thus structures and their articulation are "embedded" in Gubrium's scheme.

Gubrium has outlined an approach to a problem critical to all fieldwork: How does one pin down meaning to a context and locate it within structures? The central task of symbolic analysis is the differentiation of meaning in social contexts, and we have here sufficient guidelines and examples to set an agenda.

Peter K. Manning
John Van Maanen
Marc L. Miller

PREFACE

This short book is one culmination of a long series of studies of the social organization of care in human service institutions. Its particular outcome is both theoretical and methodological, being a systematic presentation of a way of analyzing field reality. While analytic, the book also offers extensive empirical illustration of its concepts and arguments.

Over the years, the series of studies has shifted its analytic emphasis several times. It started with the documentation of the "worlds" of care embedded in a single nursing home and was thus oriented to more or less structured means of interpreting the care experience (Gubrium, 1975). It moved on to a description of interpretive processes in a residential treatment center for emotionally disturbed children and, consequently, highlighted the flux of related experiences (Buckholdt and Gubrium, 1985 [1979]). Next, it presented the impact of audience accountability on the description of treatment, care, and recovery in a physical rehabilitation hospital and, as a result, again stressed the organizational limits of interpretation (Gubrium and Buckholdt, 1982a). Finally, it reported the "reality work" entailed in sustaining the margins of the pathological and the normal in the Alzheimer's disease experience, thereby placing the tense relation between structure and process at the center of its message (Gubrium, 1986a). As a reflection on the series, this book is an analytic appreciation of the inexorable linkage between structure and process, locating method in, and around, their connection.

I am grateful to a number of colleagues and friends for reading and commenting on the manuscript—to R. Satyanarayana for continual support and critical inquiry; to John Van Maanen for incisive comments on the argument; to David Silverman for a sympathetic reading and feedback; to Gale Miller and James Holstein for collaborative commiseration from the Marquette branch of the "school"; and to Hernan Vera for careful and helpful advice on the presentation.

I also owe a debt of gratitude to the two institutions that housed the writing and revision of the book. Marquette University's Institute for Family Studies provided an environment conducive to research and

8

writing. I thank my longtime colleague and research partner, David Buckholdt, for making possible my affiliation with the institute. The University of Florida's sociology department offered support by enthusiastically receiving "one of those" qualitative types into its midst and appreciating, not distancing itself from, a methodological stranger.

And, of course, last but not least, there was and continues to be the collective contribution of that daily triumvirate: Pence, Lin Z, and the Cake.

Jaber Gubrium
Gainesville, Florida

ANALYZING FIELD REALITY

JABER GUBRIUM
University of Florida

1. INTRODUCTION

By trade, philosophers are inclined to contemplate the nature of reality. Theirs are the age-old questions: What is real? How do we know it? What ought to be done about it? The answers have ranged from attempts to actually pinpoint ultimate truths to dissolving truth itself in its own investigation. Not only ancient, philosophy is also a noble enterprise, the systematic investigation of the most basic tenets of being.

Philosophy's analytic primacy has kept it rather distant from most of our lives. There is the discourse that philosophers engage and there are the everyday concerns that challenge the rest of us. While we ostensibly all attend to the same world of being, our interests in it seem widely separated. Indeed, the professionalization of philosophical discourse has so widened the gap that philosophical activity makes its truths virtually unavailable to any but insiders. C. P. Snow's (1959) distinction between what he called the "two cultures" of humanistic and scientific interpretation seems equally applicable to the differences between philosophical commentary and everyday matters.

This short book addresses the gap. Rather than taking for granted the distinction between philosophical discourse and everyday life, it attempts to reveal the philosophical wherewithal of common men, women, boys, and girls, as they routinely take up the very questions raised by the ancients. It is not so much about formal philosophical systems or professional philosophers, as it presents a way of appreciating everyone's enduring philosophical engagement.

The study of everyday life gives careful attention to the details of interpretation and circumstance, to the minutiae and horizons of experience. It requires both tools of the trade and a method of analysis. Among the tools are procedures for establishing rapport, gathering field

9

data, and managing role relationships, as ▓▓ as departure strategies. A method of analysis, in contrast, is not so much technical as it concerns interpretation—an analytic orientation to everyday life. This book deals with method. It is not about the mechanics of fieldwork, but how to convey the field's everyday realities and its members' common philosophical engagement.

Everyday Philosophy

As a point of departure, consider some bits and pieces of my experience with the gap, episodes that serve to cast doubt on it. At first glance, the episodes hardly seem worthy of being termed *philosophical*. Yet a measure of terminological indulgence and patience with the mundane expands the philosophical horizons of those willing to be witnesses. Although the episodes are drawn from settings where I have studied people with a variety of troubles—from senility to emotional disturbance and spinal cord injuries—they reflect the philosophical minutiae of everyday life in general.

While we take it that a central and urgent philosophical question is "What is real?" how often have we all heard both acquaintances and strangers pose and contend with it? On one of many similar occasions, I witnessed children argue the question at Cedarview, a residential treatment center for emotionally disturbed boys and girls (Buckholdt and Gubrium, 1985 [1979]).

Three boys, aged 9 and 10, sat in their dormitory room (cottage) in animated conversation about firecrackers. At first, I overheard them as I sat reading comic books with several other boys in an adjacent room. I listened intently when one of the three boys, Gary, firmly asked Tom, "Can you really get firecrackers from your brother?" Tom shouted sarcastically, "Really!" What followed was a chain of now glib and now accusatory exchanges that played on the word *really*. Gary and a third boy, Bill, pressed Tom to tell the truth "or else," asking Tom whether he was "just kidding" or had actually gotten cherry bombs, a much sought after explosive. When Tom snidely blurted, "Really, really, really," the other two boys jostled Tom and joined in choruses of "no you didn't" and "you're lying."

As center staff members were in the habit of investigating jostlings accompanied by raised voices, I casually walked into the cottage. Gary turned to me and demanded that I make Tom tell the truth. The mood was as much lighthearted as it was tense. I asked Tom what he had been saying and Tom repeated his claim that he could get cherry bombs from his brother and, what was more, could get them whenever he desired. It was a timely claim since the Fourth of July was a mere two weeks away. Firecrackers seemed to be in the center's very atmosphere, both figuratively and literally.

I might have dismissed the boys' exchange in the way both the children and the staff often did, as just so much "bull," or, if warranted, I might have attempted to contain what could have become a so-called blowup. But as the three boys continued to talk and argue, it occurred to me that, in their own way, they were contending with the question "What is real?" The snide chains of "no you didn't" hurled about were not merely contentious or simply manners of speaking, but the fallout of assertion and justification. "Really, really, really" was not just Tom's tauntingly insistent claim, but a challenge leading to a demand for evidence.

Both Gary and Bill insisted that Tom offer proof for his assertion, as Gary colorfully commanded, "Okay, wiseass, put up or shut up!" Tom drew two ladyfingers from his pocket, which were less powerful firecrackers than cherry bombs. When he offered them as proof, Gary refused to believe him and shouted, "Look, man, I know what I see and those ain't cherry bombs!" This launched a round of exchanges centering on how Tom could "prove it," as each boy put it. Again, the exchanges signaled something besides a boyhood disagreement, for the exchanges oscillated between two tacit "theories" of proof, one demonstrative and one inferential. Gary insisted that one had to be "really stupid" to believe what he hadn't actually seen. Tom contended that the fact that he had the ladyfingers and an older brother who all admittedly knew could get "all kinds of stuff" made it evident that he, Tom, was "for real," as the boys often put it. In their separate usages, the two "theories" virtually urged their respective contenders to make good on successive assertions and rebuttals. Indeed, if the exchanges had not been so vivid and were distilled of their spokespersons into barebones contentions, I might have easily found myself not in the middle of argumentative boys but bold-faced rhetorics.

It struck me that there was much that was philosophical here. Yes, the boys were speaking their minds and hearts in the dormitory of a treatment center, which could cast a pathological light on their conduct. Yes, it was the kind of exchange that, save for its particulars, one encountered daily at Cedarview. All the same, there were discursive structures informing the exchanges, systems that made it seem that whoever chose to concertedly take up their logics—whether these particular boys, girls, or others in or out of Cedarview—the exchanges would be more or less played out as expected, for better or worse. It occurred to me that what might be called everyday philosophical systematics tacitly sorted out for the boys how each would choose to deal with the immediate questions before them—what was real and how to prove it. While the boys keenly articulated their contentions and artfully validated them according to their separate understandings of proof and from bits and pieces of their own experiences, their exchanges were not merely more or less reasoned spirals of interpretation, but structured ones. In effect, the related discursive structures available to the boys were as much to blame for what did, or what would, transpire in their exchange as the boys' intentions and activity.

When I casually mentioned the firecracker exchange to a friendly Cedarview social worker, the social worker was amused and added that it was a familiar story. When I repeated the story to a Cedarview teacher who had several children of her own, she, too, recognized the events and, indeed, exclaimed that she could have predicted exactly what each Cedarview boy would have said in turn as the exchange unfolded. The familiarity did not as much serve to trivialize my discoveries in the firecracker exchange as it suggested to me that the social worker and teacher were picking up on the "systematics" of what I reported, on means of understanding the seemingly obvious events described. In their own ways, the social worker's and teacher's responses informed me that discoverable systems of discourse or exchange guided and, to the extent they were discerned, made predictable the boys' course of interaction. I came to know that, for some, what was said to be predictable was also termed inevitable in the circumstance, which implied that it was perhaps not the boys as such, their intentions, or material objects that got them into trouble, as it was their collective engagement of particular logics. Neither these three boys nor others always risked getting into trouble when they were together, nor did firecrackers always suggest delinquency.

When I discussed the firecracker episode at greater length with both the teacher and the social worker, I discovered that the "systematics" I had earlier shared with them had additional interpretations. While each was amused by the boys' rationales, the teacher and social worker had their own ideas about the realities at stake in the exchange. The two staff members drew links between the boys' comparative credibility and what they attributed to their characters. Concurring with the teacher, the social worker explained that if Tom hadn't been such a chronic liar, she would have probably believed him and kept "an eye" on him lest he really did bring cherry bombs into the building. The teacher added that Tom was a "real braggart," too, just like his older brother, and that the other boys knew it. The teacher explained that this prompted the boys never to trust Tom's boasting but to want immediate proof of his claims.

The social worker's and teacher's framing of Tom as a chronic liar structured their appreciation of Tom's conduct. Other staff members differed, seeing Tom as a conniver, one who usually made good on his assertions, but at a profit. In the latter view, Tom was not as much a liar as a keen bargainer. The difference, of course, affected judgments of, and reactions to, Tom's conduct and assertions.

As far as everyday philosophy is concerned, the point of highlighting the systematic, tacit structures of understanding is that we seem able to interpret the exchange and its commentaries only when we discern structures. What Tom, Bill, and Gary were "really" doing, on the one hand, and what Cedarview staff members said they were "actually up to," on the other, were understood not so much from the actual words spoken by the boys, the physical evidence, or the unfolding events, but by way of the systems of interpretation guiding the task. Taking a kind of philosophical curiosity into the field revealed virtual philosophers at work, plying their systems in search of valid knowledge of the everyday realities of interest to them.

Such was part of an evolving appreciation of everyday philosophy. What I was seeing in episodes like the firecracker exchange and staff members' considerations of its meaning were what might be referred to as their logics-in-use. The boys were putting to use discernible means of contending with what they spoke of as the "really real" and making good on claims of having "proven it." Staff members did likewise in their interpretations of the boys' claims. As they put the respective logics to use—demonstrably, inferentially, and otherwise—they simultaneously and systematically became engulfed in their own contentions as they now challenged or committed themselves to rationally make good on their positions. In a word, *structure* was evident in every bit and piece of the exchanges, as well as in commentaries upon the exchanges, just as it was more or less obvious to each child and staff member as they dealt with each other.

Still, to speak of reality structures—ways of structuring everyday experience—as meaningfully forming the exchanges would seem to shortchange the fact that the boys and staff members used different structures to deal with the questions challenging them. In another word, they *articulated* the structures in different ways, building various bridges between apparent things and events, on one side, and what the latter could be, on the other. There were times when Tom cast aside inferential assertions and himself claimed that only someone "stupid enough" would believe what he had not seen for himself, just as there were occasions when Gary's assertions were guided by Tom's earlier sense of proof. Staff members, likewise, articulated varied structures of understanding. It was as if the field settings studied, only one of which was Cedarview, were peopled by everyday philosophers with an open stock of systematic resources—structures—for making sense of things and events, not wholly governed by the structures but variously and skillfully applying selected logics according to circumstance.

The Problem of Method

Having made a brief case for the philosopher in everyday life, we are left with the problem of how to analyze his or her actions. In the preceding episodes, Tom, Bill, Gary, and the staff members were not just behaving, they were simultaneously making sense of their conduct. Our aim, as analysts of their actions, is to formulate a method for making their interpretations sociologically intelligible.

This contrasts with another approach, which I shall mention only briefly. If, under the best conditions, we could treat conduct as virtually announcing its meaning, there would be no problem of interpretation, but, rather, one of another kind. For example, if we could somehow discern what Tom, Gary, and Bill were really up to, such as either a ruse or a concrete bargain, separate from their own and others' interpretations, we could virtually observe their "real" intentions. If this could be accomplished, the only kind of problem we would encounter in the process would be the mistakes we made in discerning what otherwise was apparent. If we made no mistakes of this sort, we could say that we had derived an "objective," "positive," or "neutral" account of behavior. In other words, it could be claimed that (1) we had obtained a depiction of the realities as they are, which (2) were separate and independent of their respective claimant's interpretations.

Let us distinguish the two types of treatment, respectively, as the interpretive and positivist approaches to everyday reality and elaborate the former. Some take Weber (1947: 88) as having defined the subject matter of the interpretive approach, calling it "action." Weber wrote that "in 'action' is included all human behavior when and in so far as the acting individual attaches a subjective meaning to it." Regarding the

Cedarview episodes, an interpretive approach would take Tom's, Gary's, and Bill's actions as located in the ways they and others assigned meaning or reality to their behavior. As such, reality is a kind of linkage between a possible way of defining something, on the one hand, and that something, on the other. It should be borne in mind that reality is neither one or the other, but a linkage of the two. Accordingly, while the phrase "subjective meaning" is used in Weber's definition, the interpretive approach is not subjectivistic, for it pertains to the attachment of meaning. This focuses attention on the public practice of interpretation, not on some private, mental process.

What Weber meant by subjective meaning was the meaning of something for the subject, as we might have distinguished the reality of the firecracker episode according to Tom, Gary, Bill, Cedarview staff members, or combinations thereof, such as therapeutic versus administrative staff. Because Weber's project was largely historical, the subjective meanings he considered fell into civilizational and societal categories. For example, Weber read different forms of action from the religious behavior of Western as opposed to oriental civilizations, especially as the behavior had different meanings for, and consequences in, economic development (Weber, 1958). Our project, while informed by Weber's interpretive approach, is focused on a different scale: interactive fields. The field reality under consideration spreads over the circumstances and organizations that provide participants with the problem of interpreting everyday life. Action is the interpretive work undertaken in the process, circumscribed by the subjective meanings available to those concerned, on the one hand, and the things and events they consider, on the other.

What Weber termed subjective meanings, I call "structures." I have chosen to use the term rather than Weber's phrase because, as I shall show later, experience in analyzing field realities indicates that the realities are more situationally and organizationally circumscribed, more fixed, than the phrase "subjective meaning" would suggest. In that regard, structures are not only public and practical resources for assigning meaning, discernible in action and interaction, but are socially organized as well. One might guess, for example, that a behavior assessment in a psychoanalytically oriented institution would highlight the fundamental reality of deep and covert mental processes over the visible activity officially scrutinized at Cedarview.

Circumstances, formal organizations, and organizational settings all provide participants with structures for interpreting their own and others' lives. Following Geertz (1973: 12), I take "culture [to] consist of socially established structures of meaning." Accordingly, formal organizations, for example, combine both official and unofficial structures to compose organizational culture. Cedarview was committed officially to a behavioral approach to emotional disturbance and had in place a complex behavior modification program. This, of course, did not mean that other interpretive structures did not inform the Cedarview staff's actions. At Cedarview, depth psychology and Freudianisms were frequently in evidence. Nonetheless, whatever structures served to interpret the children's conduct, for reporting purposes, descriptions were submitted to regulating and funding agencies in behavioral terminology. We might take it, then, that the formality of settings does not as much specify available structures for interpreting behavior as it serves to distinguish and present a public identity in accordance with a particular structure.

Methodological Stance

Because we locate the meaningful realities of everyday life in action, in the linkage between structures, things, and behaviors, as sociologists we stand twice-removed from the objects and events that concern us (Schutz, 1963a, 1963b, 1970). The people or folk whose lives we study are once-removed in that their concerns are meaningfully encountered by way of their own interpretations. Sociologists are twice-removed in that they interpret the interpretations of those studied. This methodological stance is summarized in Figure 1.1.

Let us consider Figure 1.1's components in relation to the episodes presented earlier. The reference "folk," rather than respondents, informants, or subjects, is used for people because they are described in terms of native orientations to the things and events of concern to them. Folk include Tom, Gary, Bill, Cedarview staff members, and others engaged in the process of figuring realities in diverse domains of their own worlds. Our attitude toward them resembles the anthropologist's stance in the observation of a world of people whose behaviors are made visible through analysis, but validly interpreted only through native categories of understanding. What is real for Tom, Gary, Bill, and others is informed by means of the structures they bring to bear on the question. Whether Tom is actually a wily purveyor of fireworks or a liar depends as much on the ways of discerning Tom as it does on the concrete evidence available. We might ask, for example, what it means when Tom pulls a few ladyfingers from his pocket for others to see. This

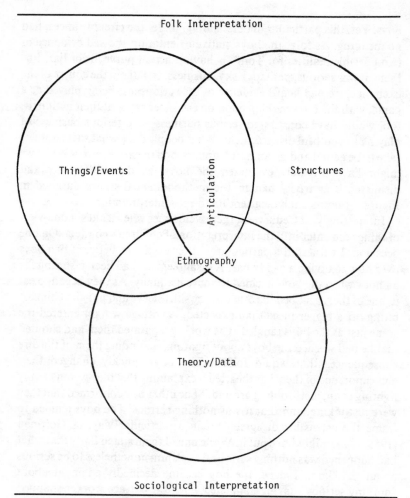

Figure 1.1: Structure/Articulation

is another way of asking what the reality of the objects and event is in the episode. In short, what is Tom really doing? The question is not merely academic, for it is the sort of native query whose answer, at Cedarview for one place, will determine whether Tom is making progress in emotional self-control, is still delinquent, or will be dismissed merely as "full of hot air."

As outside observers of the episode, we might have thought that what was actually occurring was just one more kid's game among delinquent boys. Yet, this particular understanding, under the circumstances, had no meaning. As folk, the boys' native orientation showed evidence of two possible realities for Tom's behavior: actual purveyor or liar. For them, it was serious, perhaps risky, business. If, later in the course of the exchange, we had heard evidence of the seriousness being played as a game, with the boys making good on the latter sense of their action, it, too, would have constituted serious business—the serious business of playing at youthful disagreement. What people do is what they, not we, take to be actual and meaningful, understood in native terms. While we might have privately evaluated the boys' conduct differently and dismissed it as trivial banter, the methodological stance outlined in Figure 1.1 limits analytic attention to folk interpretation.

Interestingly, at Cedarview, there were times when a kid's-game-view of things did enter into the interpretation of children's conduct. On one occasion, I witnessed a particularly bitter exchange between two boys over how to divide a candy bar. A disagreement had been festering for an hour when the boys decided to share it equally. As they began to eat it, one of them grabbed the other by the shirt sleeve and punched him for biting off a bigger piece than expected. A cottage worker entered the scene just as the boys tangled. The worker separated them and shouted that he had warned the boys about fighting, reminding them of the dire consequences that would follow. The boys quickly changed their demeanor, one of them lightheartedly explaining that they weren't really fighting at all, just "fooling around." The other boy confirmed that they were just joking, and that it was nothing serious. The boys teamed to frame the ostensible disagreement in a particular way, as Goffman (1959, 1974) might have put it. While one of them stated flatly that what had happened was nothing serious, I took him nonetheless to be serious about the claim. Indeed, the boy became decidedly adamant about "nothing serious" having happened when the cottage worker snapped that he didn't believe a word of it.

As far as our methodological stance is concerned, evidence of folk interpretation is drawn from the flow and substance of what people say and claim about things and events. I took it that there was no "kid's game" articulated in the preceding episode until the boys themselves teamed together and cast their behavior for the cottage worker accordingly. This, of course, does not mean that "kidding" was not available to the boys for structuring their behavior (or, as Weber might have put it, for "attaching meaning to it"), only that kidding was not continuously apparent in their actions and, thereby, not always the practical reality informing the exchange.

This suggests that the emerging reality of behavior hinges on both articulation and available structures, bringing us to the methodological implications of the relationship between structure and articulation. The intersecting circles of Figure 1.1, in particular the top two, are meant to convey the impossibility of completely separating their respective domains. Articulation is part of what Giddens (1979) called "structuration." As Giddens wrote, "Structure thus is not to be conceptualized as a barrier to action, but as essentially involved in its production" (p. 70). When the boys tangled over sharing a candy bar, their behavior could have meant many things. Ironically, describing it as a tangle in the first place, as a way of introducing the point I am now making, necessarily violated the methodological stance we are taking. Yet it was a self-conscious violation in that it was done only as a necessary beginning for eventual appropriation to folk structures. In short, I called it a tangle to turn our attention empirically toward something we then were ready to turn away from, toward folk interpretation. In this regard, even the bottom circle intersects the other two, schematizing the partial overlay of all interpretive domains depicted in the figure. As such, neither structure nor articulation are conclusively clear in the field. Analysis proceeds incrementally with the aim of making visible the native practice of clarification, from one domain of experience to another, structure upon structure.

For the present purpose, let us concentrate on the top two circles and orient to the candy bar incident as a folk world of things and events pulsating with possible meanings. They "pulsate" because their realities are apparent, not decided. Our methodological stance cues us toward discerning structures to be articulated in the actions of those concerned. As we analytically enter the scene, we might cautiously presume a fight. We then hear a fight assigned to their activity by the boys themselves or, at the least, tentatively take a fight as occurring based on a common conception of what a fight looks and sounds like. As sociologists, we use what our common culture provides as ways to assign meaning to the events under consideration. At the same time, as noted earlier, we are ready to withdraw a tentative interpretation as events unfold.

As the cottage worker enters the scene and declares a fight to be occurring, our tentative assessment of what was going on is confirmed for the time being. When we hear the boys argue that the incident was not a real fight, but just kidding, we empirically amend our initial assessment as partial (and possibly partisan). It is only now, with the alternate framing, that we recognize the initial interpretation as a structure, now discerning two structures for articulating events—one structuring the incident as a fight and the other as kidding around. The difference, of course, is more than a mere language game, while it is nonetheless linguistic, for it is the prevailing structure that will guide further articulation of past and future things and events related to the incident, not to mention practical, localized consequences for those concerned.

One might very well raise the issue of power here. Our methodological stance suggests that this be considered in terms of the rhetoric of assertion, claims, and counterclaims, rather than objective force or authority. Force and authority themselves are subject to claims and counterclaims. For example, while cottage workers are mostly bigger and stronger than the children, as well as officially charged with managing the children's behavioral programming in the dormitory, the cottage workers also are concerned with "not pushing things too far," lest a continual battle of definitional wits ensue. What this could mean in the candy bar incident is that a cottage worker who insisted on seeing a fight where joking was counterclaimed might risk what at Cedarview and other places are called "overreacting," "being too rigid," "using poor judgment," and/or "not being well enough aware of things," among a host of articulations of articulation. What power or prevalence is, is itself something structured or framed. Consequently, methodologically, we might well think of power or authority as a feature of the relationship of structure and articulation rather than as a limiting condition on action (see Foucault, 1981 [1977], 1972 [1969]).

It is the persistent interrelationship of articulation and structure that compels us to specify the term "action" beyond Weber's definition. Recall that Weber defined action as the attaching of subjective meaning to behavior. Referring to the firecracker exchange and applying Weber's definition, we would conclude that Tom's conduct and possession of ladyfingers would represent whatever meaning was assigned to Tom's behavior. Tom would really be either a liar or an actual purveyor of fireworks, depending on how his behavior was interpreted. Some years ago, W. I. Thomas (1966) approached experiential realities in much the same way, arguing that if situations were defined as real, they would be real in their consequences. The point of both Weber's and Thomas's contentions is that, to understand experience, we must set aside a positivist orientation to things and events and appreciate their meanings for those concerned. It is the meanings or definitions of things and events, as Thomas suggested, that informs and guides action and ongoing interaction. Still, while the flux of action and interaction seems to be the sense-making stuff taking place in the firecracker exchange and in other episodes of everyday life, it is precisely the flux feature that is lacking in Weber's and Thomas's otherwise useful approaches.

People not only attach meaning to their respective behaviors, but repeatedly engage the task, now categorizing one thing or event as real and now reclassifying an earlier categorization by way of forthcoming sentiments and opinions on the matter. As such, folk seem to use historical experience as much as they are beset by it. At the same time, meanings are attached out of diverse structures of understanding. For example, given that Tom is perceived as an inveterate liar, relevant features of his current behavior are taken to be signs of another habitual ruse. This structuring may or may not compete with other under-standings for informing the articulation of events as they occur. Meaning assigned in the course of interaction comes to be an object in its own right when it is subject to the question of whether it really is a viable option. For example, having defined the ladyfingers as yet another sign of Tom's habitual lying, the possibility that Tom may be using his well-known habit to keep others from prying into an actual cache of cherry bombs leads those concerned to attach a different meaning to the ladyfingers, now being potential signs of what they were not. One hears the potential restructuring of events and reassignment of meaning to the firecrackers when Gary asks Bill, "How do we know he [Tom] really isn't putting us on and really does have the cherry bombs?" and Bill answers, "Yeah, like maybe he's doing a reverse con-job on us."

I have chosen to use the term *articulation* in place of action because the attaching of meaning of which Weber spoke, as observed in face-to-face fields, is so vividly processual and practical. The attaching is not merely a matter of exercising the application of a definition, as Thomas had it, but involves enduring definitional labor. The firecracker exchange as well as commentary on the exchange, together with yet other commentaries on the commentary, are complex interpretive layers concerning the reality under consideration. Accordingly, when we observe and hear Tom, Gary, Bill, and others address the real meaning of the boys' behavior, we encounter them as not only concerned with what they concretely confront, but, at the same time, as they figure the meaning of what is seen and heard. To use the analogy applied at the start, they are simultaneously and persistently both the concrete agents of their actions and the actions' everyday philosophers. Each attempt to discern what really is going on is also the work of addressing the questions of what is to be taken as real, how to settle that question, and what ought to be done about whatever is decided.

Garfinkel (1967) was a pioneer in the study of articulation. He referred to it by a rather different term—*ethnomethodology*—virtually the philosophical modus operandi of everyday life. Ethnomethodology pertains to the practical methods of reasoning used by people to sort and assign meaning to experience, as we described action in the preceding episodes. While the ethnomethodological contribution to the study of everyday life is very useful, ethnomethodology has so emphasized the processual, articulative feature of folk interpretation as to overshadow its substantive structures. In the firecracker exchange, the "methods" Tom, Gary, Bill, and others used to decide what Tom was really doing would be highlighted at the expense of the available options (structures) for defining what Tom is. In its most radical form, ethnomethodology glosses the latter altogether, attempting to analyze structure as communication itself.

In the approach to field realities being developed here, I give equal status to structures. Structures are not treated as independent of articulation nor as epiphenomenal, but, as the top two intersecting circles of Figure 1.1 suggest, as partially independent. For example, we know from observation at Cedarview that Tom is likely to be conceived as either a guileful teller of the truth, a chronic liar, or even pathological, which one Tom really is depending on how the three means of structuring his conduct are articulated in relation to ongoing events in and out of the firecracker exchange. It does matter for Tom, Gary, Bill, and others that there are these particular substantive options (structures), just as it matters that the structure engaged and secured will depend on the everyday philosophical wherewithal of those concerned.

Structures matter in their own right because, despite articulative acumen, settings do not all provide their participants with the same understandings of experience. For example, should Tom's family be imbued with what some would call the "family myth" of Tom being a born liar, the everyday philosophical juggling of its members would continually, if not exquisitely, articulate Tom's behavior accordingly, something that would not necessarily occur in another setting. Laing (1969), Laing and Esterson (1964), Anderson and Bagarozzi (1983), Bagarozzi and Anderson (1982), Jackson (1973), Ferreira (1963), and Gubrium (1987a) have provided analyses of families along this line, focusing on how domestic understandings (called "family myths" or "family fictions") structure the reality of members' behaviors. Insofar as organizations and their professionals, such as Cedarview and its staff members, formally claim adherence to particular structures, there are official and accountable realities to articulate (see Dingwall and Strong, 1985; Silverman, 1970, 1985). The fact that the boys in the firecracker exchange engaged each other at Cedarview brought their behavior within the purview of emotional disturbance as an official interpretive structure.

The ethnography and component theory and data of the lower circle of Figure 1.1 is the sociological activity of describing folk interpretation, as the etymology of the term *ethnography* infers. For analytic purposes, ethnography sorts the simultaneous articulation of, and folk engagement with, meaningful realities. While Tom, Bill, Gary, and others focus their attentions on the apparent objects and events of concern to them, as ethnographers we witness and analyze the social organization of their attention, action, and interaction. This is not to say that people do not concern themselves with the ways they attend to the realities of everyday life. They do, but when they do so, they take the realities to be among the things and objects of practical interest to them. Of course, folk attention to life can be extended into countless layers of concern over concern. However complex the layering, as ethnographers, the focus of attention is on folk engagements with reality, whether the topic of interest be articulation itself or an ostensible observable like the meaning of ladyfingers. The methodological stance links an interpretive under-standing of folk reality with the ethnographic task of documenting both articulation and structure, aiming to make visible both the flux and the limits of experience.

The interdependence assigned to structure and articulation has been variously emphasized in interpretive approaches to everyday life. Some have chosen to give analytic primacy to structures, others to articulation, as we shall see in the next chapter.

2. FIELD REALITY: ORIENTATIONS

The study of field realities is sometimes called "qualitative sociology." While it is usually distinguished from a positivist approach, qualitative sociology is nonetheless not a unitary enterprise. This chapter conveys the variety. The three orientations presented—structural, articulative, and practical—show how analytic focus provides different visions of field reality. The everyday philosophers we hear and observe in fieldwork are not alone in conveying meaning to us; ethnography itself engages the communication.

There is a historical argument in the presentation. Structural ethnography represents the tradition of the field, articulative ethnography the reaction. As I frame it, practical ethnography is the synthesis. As Dingwall and Strong (1985), Silverman (1985), and Hammersley and Atkinson (1983) imply, following the important contribution of ethnomethodology (articulative ethnography) to understanding everyday life, it is time to reconsider the place of structure in folk understanding.

Structural Ethnography

When ethnography orients to folk structures, the articulation of everyday realities is deemphasized. In this view, field realities are located in the existing subjective meanings for interpreting experience. In the episodes described earlier, rather than explicating how Tom, Gary, and Bill work out the realities of their exchange, or on how staff members' considerations of the boys' conduct serve to discern realities in their own right, we depict what the subjective meanings are of their respective actions and how the meanings are organized.

A classic ethnography of this type is Whyte's (1955) study of the street life of young men in an Italian slum. As any good ethnographer would, Whyte was careful not to use prevailing popular opinion about street life to interpret the actions of the "corner boys" he observed. Indeed, one purpose of his study was to challenge the common view that the habitues of the streets and corners were devoid of moral life, without rules, rights, duties, and obligations. Orienting his observations to the subjective meaning of everyday life in "Cornerville," Whyte found a complex array of native understandings that served to structure the young men's behavior. Whyte's account, in his book *Street Corner Society,* described the structure in detail.

Returning to Tom, Gary, Bill, and others at Cedarview, an ethnography orienting to structure would, as Whyte's did, convey what the children and others understood their behaviors to mean. While we might have easily scoffed at their conduct as a mere kid's game and dismissed it, careful attention to the subjective meaning of Cedarview conduct would show that no one in a residential treatment center glibly dismisses just any potential "blowup" as a mere kid's game. Indeed, if we were attentive to what Cedarview folk said about their daily affairs, we would notice that all children's behavior on the center's premises was potential grist for emotional disturbance. Yet, we also would have found that, while all the behavior can potentially signal disturbance, there are discernible rules for when and where such interpretation takes place.

It is important to emphasize that the rules are the native ways by which Cedarview folk attend to children's conduct. This means that, whatever Tom, Bill, and Gary do and say to each other, their behavior is taken to be a sign of emotional disturbance only when and where those concerned choose to attach that kind of meaning to it. Otherwise, the behavior is something else, has a different reality.

Let us consider the interpretation of two Cedarview boys' behavior, Jim's and Mike's, in a particularly exciting and tense basketball game. Jim and Mike were on opposite teams and, in the final minutes of the game, became very aggressive. Without directly fouling the other, each was especially wary about the other's moves. One of the cottage workers remarked that the two were "really psyching each other out" as the score evened and time ran out. At one point, Mike's quick movement to retrieve a wayward ball started Jim shouting. Mike caught the ball before it went out of bounds, threw it, and missed the basket. As the game ended, the two boys got into a verbal battle over whether Jim's shouting had unfairly caused Mike to miss a basket that could have won the game. The disagreement, which was heated, did not quite lead to blows, but it lasted throughout the day.

Several staff members had either watched or heard about the game and, the next day, casually discussed the Jim-Mike episode. One staff member, a special education teacher, remarked that Jim's shouting had made Mike so nervous that Mike missed the sort of shot he normally successfully completed. The teacher added that Jim was a "real clown" on the court and could "psych out" anyone, even the best players. There was agreement all around until a cottage worker raised the fairness issue, as Mike himself had the day before. As the conversation unfolded, the staff members, in turn, took up one or the other boy's cause. On this occasion, Jim's and Mike's behaviors were contenders for judgments of fairness and good sportsmanship.

I heard the same episode considered in an entirely different situation, again at Cedarview. In a treatment team review, a child's behavior is formally addressed in terms of the emotional disturbance it shows. Conduct is evaluated according to its pathology, targeted treatment goals, programming, and course of progress. When Jim's behavior management was discussed in a review, the teacher who had commented on what a "real clown" Jim was now described him as always being "hotheaded," exemplifying it with reference to the endgame episode.

Others heard a message of pathology in the remark, in keeping with the therapeutic tenor of the review. On this occasion, the teacher used Jim's endgame behavior for different purposes. Jim's shouting, while the "same" behavior considered earlier, was a different act. Indeed, it was evident that the subjective meanings understood to be formally at hand in discussing the children's behaviors served to place all behavior within the framework of emotional disturbance. It was not that all the conduct suddenly became emotionally disturbed under the circumstances but that particular behaviors were now considered for whether they were or were not disturbed, and if so, to what degree, and what should be done about it.

Comparison of the two situations shows how the process of folk interpretation is guided by discernible rules that organize the applicability of interpretive structures. In team reviews and similar meetings, we find that a prominent structuring centers on emotional disturbance; outside of these situations, we observe that such framings are less prominent, others being highlighted.

Structures, of course, did spill over situational bounds. Reviews of emotional disturbance at Cedarview, for example, sometimes abided nontherapeutic interpretation, like sportsmanship. Casual circumstance sometimes generated framings of emotional disturbance. When such spillovers did occur, they were recognized as such readily enough by those concerned and regularly used to appropriately adjust circumstances, as when convivial talk of "real clowning" was entertained in the course of what was otherwise a treatment team review, and then foreclosed to "get back to business." Cautions informed by spillovers were a means of circumstantial and interpretive control.

As far as articulation was concerned, the control was both constructive and destructive of field realities. Structural ethnography tends to gloss spillovers and the circumstantial control activity containing them. Instead, structural ethnography classifies and highlights the social organization and distribution of subjective meanings as native and diverse field realities. It is less concerned with the process by which the field realities emerge, are secured, and transformed, than it is with cataloging their forms and relationships in time and space.

Articulative Ethnography

Spillovers and interpretive control phenomena appeal to a different ethnographic orientation, one centered on articulation. The approach has been taken in important directions by ethnomethodological fieldworkers. From Garfinkel's (1967) work with organizational records to Cicourel's, Kitsuse's, and others' (1963) studies of educational decision making, Wieder's (1973) analysis of the "snitching" code, and conversational analysts' work on turn-taking and other rules of talk (see Sudnow, 1972), the focus of analysis has been on how members of situations assemble reasonable understandings of the things and events of concern to them and, thereby, realize them as objects of everyday life. The "how" of folk interpretation is emphasized over the "what," ethnomethods over substance.

While articulative ethnography takes an interest in the subjective meaning of behavior, it stresses the native analytic work and categorization practices that inform action. The aim is to derive rules of reality-construction (see Cicourel, 1972). But once either the rules are specified or the sense of rule-use is highlighted, the concrete things and events of everyday life are returned to the background of analysis and displaced by further ethnographic attention to articulation. Because structures take a back seat to articulation, ethnographic accounts may read like whirlwinds of layer upon layer of native interpretive activity. Indeed, a favorite ethnomethodological image is the reflexive-reality metaphor shown in Escher's picture *Drawing Hands*, where one hand is drawing another, which, in turn, draws the first (see Mehan and Wood, 1975: frontispiece). Escher was a master illusionist, which the texture of some articulative ethnography suggests is an apt interpretation of field reality.

The spillover phenomenon mentioned earlier makes particularly vivid the reality-work evident in all action. In this regard, it is important to point out that while spillover might empirically highlight articulation, the ethnomethodological project is not limited to spillovers as particular slices of the empirical world. Ethnomethodology is not the theory and method of such events while different ethnographic orientations pertain to other aspects of the empirical world. Rather, ethnomethodology is a general orientation, attuned to the pervasive articulative features of everyday life. As such, it should not be taken as "triangulating" (Denzin, 1970a) or partially completing a common ethnographic project in tandem with other orientations. By its own accounts, ethnomethodology should be considered a general gloss on all experience (see Denzin, 1970b; Zimmerman and Wieder, 1970; Gallant and Kleinman, 1983; Rawls, 1985; Gallant and Kleinman, 1985). Accordingly, the spillover phenomenon highlights processes more or less evident throughout folk interpretation.

Let us return to the spillover phenomenon and Jim's endgame behavior. (I should point out that the book *Caretakers* [Buckholdt and Gubrium, 1985(1979)], which reports some of the data gathered at Cedarview, where Jim and others had been placed for treatment, is a type of ethnomethodological account. In the present context, then, the spillover as a feature of folk interpretation is discussed throughout the ethnography.) How did those concerned know what things and events were at stake as they considered and discussed Jim's endgame behavior? Keep in mind that, in articulative ethnography, the question is not whether Jim is actually a real clown or character, or really emotionally disturbed as evidenced by his "hotheaded" shouting, but how perceptions of each separate reality are articulated. While the structures "real clown" and "real emotional disturbance" are conceptual candidates for what those concerned believe was seen before their very own eyes (or, at least, heard from more or less reputable sources), in the ethnomethodological project, the structures are topics to study in their own right, not resources by which to evaluate native interpretations of Jim's conduct. As ethnomethodologists are in the habit of putting it, the question is, how do those concerned do real clown and how do they do emotional disturbance?

Because the reality of the endgame events involving Jim and Mike is taken to be an artifact of how the spillover phenomenon is resolved, what those concerned do in the process of figuring what happened structures what is taken to have occurred when Jim shouted and Mike missed the basket. It is as much what those concerned do in interpreting Jim's behavior that realizes (makes real) what he is for all practical purposes, as it is bits and pieces of Jim's activity as concrete occurrences. Where the kind of structural ethnography called "labeling theory" would see Jim's emotional disturbance in terms of how disturbance varied in the perceptions and interpretations of those concerned, articulative ethnography would tend to see the concern itself as "doing" what Jim could really be on varied occasions. The possibility that Jim's and other boys' behavior might be mistakenly labeled as disturbed when it actually was not, or misperceived as normal when it actually was deviant, would apply only in labeling theory (see Becker, 1963: 20). As will be shown shortly, the possibilities would present themselves only in articulative ethnography as a layer of concern with the reality of Jim's behavior.

Consider a team review in which Jim's endgame behavior was discussed. In deciding how far Jim had progressed on his program to reduce "hotheadedness," his teacher recounted the endgame shouting and its subsequent very tense moments as "proof positive" that Jim had not progressed as expected. The teacher pointed out that, together with other recent "blowups," the incident clearly indicated that Jim needed further treatment and guidance. Other team members added evidence of their own and it was concluded that the hotheadedness supported a picture of festering disturbance, a very volatile child who was capable of acting out at any time.

Yet, within the review, there were moments that showed that the final decision was far from a foregone conclusion. It was not just a matter of being right or wrong about the meaning of Jim's conduct. At one point, the social worker altered the tenor of the review when he smiled and remarked, in semididactic fashion, that one had to give Jim credit for really knowing how to psych out an opponent. The remark momentarily slipped the reality under consideration from being a feature of Jim's underlying disturbance to being an aspect of Jim's characteristically skilled and wily sportsmanship. Momentarily, the team reviewers were bantering raconteurs of what they had witnessed or heard mentioned. Each spoke the discourse of fair and unfair play, defending or disparaging Jim's shouting according to their respective senses of athletic proficiency.

While argument and proof supported a separate reality for the moment, it soon ended as the social worker looked at his watch and noted that the team better get back to business. The comment simultaneously signaled two layers of team members' experience: the division between members' official work and its nonofficial interstices, on the one hand, and the relation between what we have called articulation and structure, on the other. As far as the first was concerned, in "getting back to business," team members returned to what they then took to be the real matters at hand, what Cedarview was officially chartered to care for and treat—emotional disturbance. Regarding the second layer, team members could be seen articulating the structural basis of their experience, accordingly framing their discourse and related realities. The implicit articulative rule was that, in time designated official, one perceived and took account of the presence or absence of emotional disturbance, not of sportsmanship as such. Indeed, in official time, sportsmanship became the figure, not the ground, of Jim's endgame, leading to the question of whether it was possible for an emotionally disturbed boy to act in a truly sportsman-like fashion. Getting back to business was as much about team members' return to the "doing" of emotional disturbance as it was about reverting attention to how Jim's endgame figured in his disturbance.

Official time itself was subject to articulation, yet another layer of folk interpretation. The interpretation was not as much determined by the official organization of staff activity as that official structurings of the children's conduct were actions staff took the time to do. While formal job descriptions required the staff to conduct team reviews, assessments, treatment programming, and the like, it was formal responsibility effected by those concerned. I saw official therapeutic activity vary widely in time allocation. Some ostensibly official activity was reduced to the first and last minutes of much longer, formally scheduled reviews; other official activity infringed significantly on staff members' so-called free time or time-out, where altogether different realities were often engaged.

In the team reviews, there was evidence, too, of the folk labeling mentioned earlier. Labeling theorists have usefully encouraged us, as sociologists, to attend to the processes whereby people, human service professionals especially, label those in their charge or care. Through a process of mutual identification, the labeled are not only mistakenly identified as deviant when they are not (or the reverse), but with the label's application and internalization, a new identity is forged. While articulative ethnographers might take an interpretive cue from labeling theorists, the orientation to articulation shifts the ethnographic focus from the analysis of the relationship of everyday reality to its representing categories or labels, to the descriptive organization of labels per se. We observe folk making use of labeling theory itself or its facsimiles in assigning reality to behavior.

Later in Jim's team review, participants informally tallied the number of episodes of blowing up Jim had had in the last month. When the social worker reminded the team not to forget the shouting, the teacher wondered aloud whether they should really count it, that is, tally it into Jim's blowup ratio (number of blowups per month). Cedarview's behavioral orientation and behavior modification programming involved staff members in countless quantitative assessments, the so-called baseline and postbaseline measurement of conducts such as shouting, swearing, blowing up, and acting out in general. While the assessments were ubiquitous, their completion was far from simple behavioral arithmetic, as we can begin to tell from the teacher's wondering.

The teacher's open concern was an important circumstantial turning point, for it marked a decided layering of interpretation. Before that, team members' attention, while tallying episodes of blowing up, was on recollections of Jim's recent conduct. The monthly tally progressed with each team member providing instances of inappropriate conduct recognized as blowups. Members were aided in their efforts by a variety of documents, from informal records of classroom and cottage activity to formal tallies of targeted conduct drawn from different Cedarview departments. With the teacher's open concern, team members' attention shifted from recollections of Jim's inappropriate behavior as such, to the nature of their related attention. The shift was evident in team members' concern with whether the endgame shouting was well beyond the normal confines of an excited outburst or was actually a shrewd, competitive tactic. The teacher explained that it had occurred to him that he had seen many instances of psyching out both in and out of Cedarview and had never thought of them as disturbed, only skillful.

Team members compared their definitions of shouting, arguing for and against specific views. When one specified shouting to be obvious in its sheer pitch and accompanying agitation, another asked whether the activity leading to the latter could be ignored. The arguments were not only meant to reasonably persuade but drew upon evidence from their spokespersons' own and others' related experience. Participants moved from one layer of concern with events to another as they now discussed the validity of each others' definitions and now turned directly to varied concrete recollections in support of their contentions, a virtual documentation of experience (see Garfinkel, 1967).

The layering was guided by articulation rules. When one member chose to ignore the definitional issue and get back to "what really happened," he was reminded by another that that was precisely what they were trying to figure. An extended disagreement between the two suggested that one's articulation rule accorded truth in the matter to factual determination while the other's articulation rule extended truth to considerations of how to define the factual. Indeed, yet another layering was voiced when one of them, the factual determinist, stated that the team would get nowhere if they continued to split hairs, characteristically adding that Jim was obviously emotionally disturbed and that the shouting was just another instance of what they already knew. All in all, the exchanges and commentaries rather elegantly featured the everyday philosophical turns of folk interpretation.

Interestingly, to the extent that articulative ethnography dwells on articulation at the expense of structure, it, too, analytically reflects the process of getting nowhere. The ethnomethodological project of discerning the social organization of articulation easily gets mired in the description of rule-use in layer upon layer of attention to things and events in relation to attention as such. In some forms of conversation analysis, the project becomes the study of the technical articulation rules of discourse itself: conversational turn-taking, sequencing, and the like (see Sudnow, 1972; Turner, 1974). At the same time, though, people do remind each other, just as their reminders indirectly tell us, that their actions are, after all, about real things and actual occurrences. It is the latter sense of the apparently real and its immediate, concrete urgencies that will, in the next section, inform a third orientation I shall call "practical ethnography."

Before that, though, let us return briefly to the team members' discussion of the meaning of Jim's endgame behavior. As their everyday philosophical skill came to the fore, so did their label theorizing. As mentioned earlier in distinguishing structural from articulative ethnography, labeling theorists concern themselves with the social and personal consequences of structuring things and events correctly or incorrectly. They are particularly concerned with the consequences of incorrect, especially pejorative, structuring, to which they tend to limit the term *labeling,* not usually bothering to investigate the "labeled" features of correct, or incorrect but felicitous, labeling (see Becker, 1963, chap. 2). The emphasis, understandably, follows from an enduring commitment to the "underdog" in human relations (Becker, 1967).

At one point in the team review of Jim's shouting, the teacher who had audibly wondered whether to count Jim's shouting as an instance of blowing up asked the other team members whether counting the behavior might be labeling it something it was really not. Fieldwork at Cedarview and other settings showed that the idea of labeling and the term *label* were not exclusively sociological, but also part of the cautionary culture of human service personnel and institutions. Indeed, labeling was a discernible articulation rule appropriated to the work of those who felt they were altruistically dealing in human troubles, serving to contain a professional and organizational thrust toward the pathological and therapeutic. No one, not even those who questioned the teacher's wondering over the meaning of Jim's shouting, wanted to engage in labeling. No one wanted to label even for what might appear to be a good cause, such as what a falling census might suggest staff members do in order to keep children in residence and protect jobs. At the same time, while labeling was generally considered undesirable, the vicissitudes of labeling talk itself were, for better or worse, yet another layer of concern with the very behavior upon which its spokespersons' attentions were otherwise focused.

Team members' and others' native cautiousness over, and open talk about, labeling suggests that labeling is an articulation rule. As such, an ethnographic orientation that adopts labeling as a mode of analysis risks describing only a narrow range of folk adaptations to interpretation (see Warren and Johnson, 1973). Moreover, the adoption of the labeling concept as a mode of analysis also shortchanges people's awareness and use of labeling, glossing related native discourse and judgments.

While all Cedarview personnel believed labeling to be undesirable, it was by no means clear, both there and in the other settings, which interpretive judgments were labels. Staff members also considered whether they were appropriately labeling their labels. For example, when the teacher cautioned that the team should take care not to label all of Jim's behavior as disturbed, that in the endgame Jim might have simply been putting well-honed competitive wits to work, those who stood to be accused denied that they were labeling. One of the latter stated that his categorization and tally of the shouting as disturbed was not labeling, but just squared with the facts.

The point of the last illustration is that people appear to be more philosophically astute at labeling theory than labeling theorists warrant. Native concern is not limited to the causes and consequences of implicit labeling but includes adept estimates of its very meaning and proper application to boot. Articulative ethnography provides a method for capturing the latter by sociologically casting labeling as a folk interpretive rule.

The point of elaborating the articulative activity of the endgame incident in general is to provide an example of how articulative ethnographers approach field reality. It is also a general analytic caution. An orientation to the complexities of rule-usage and articulative layering in the analysis and investigation of the experientially real— whether a shout was a sign of disturbance or a sign of skill—seems to dissolve things and events into the active considerations of those concerned. As a field reality, the shout too easily becomes its everyday philosophical engagement.

Practical Ethnography

Pervasive folk concern with concrete reality compels us, as ethnographers, to give realities more analytic credit, even while people show ample evidence of skillfully working at the meaning of meaning. There is a need for balance in the ethnographic orientation to structure and articulation. In studying a variety of human service organizations—

from nursing homes (Gubrium, 1975, 1980a, 1980b) to the residential treatment center for emotionally disturbed children (Buckholdt and Gubrium, 1985 [1979]), the physical rehabilitation hospital (Gubrium and Buckholdt, 1982a), and the Alzheimer's disease day hospital and support groups for caregivers (Gubrium, 1986a, 1986b)—I have attempted to develop a practical ethnography. Its guiding metaphor is the practitioner of everyday life, one who, together with others, engages the matter of figuring the meaning of things and events in their worlds in order to conduct the latter's concrete business. Practitioners of everyday life not only interpret their worlds but do so under discernible auspices, with recognizable agendas.

Practical ethnography contrasts with structural ethnography in that practical ethnography strikes a greater balance with articulation. While the classification and distribution of subjective meanings or structures is highlighted, there is studied attention to how classification is constructed, secured, and maintained. For example, while we might catalog the various experiential realities in a particular setting, we also attend to the ways its members assign and organize the realities in the course of dealing with related practical concerns. For the practical ethnographer, it is not enough to describe how events such as endgame shouting are subject to differential interpretations in and out of formal behavior assessments. Even within the bounds of when and where things and events are presumably construed in particular ways, people attend to both the substance of their concern and the borders of their attention. As such, the structures for Jim's shouting, for example, are not merely discernible as wily sportsmanship and emotional disturbance. Those who engage the structures also are skilled at their application; they regulate when, how, and where to use them.

The whens, hows, and wheres of usage are not so much strictly specifiable as they are worked at in the course of related everyday activity. As noted earlier, while the team members tallying Jim's recent blowups considered the endgame shouting from different angles, the way the shouting was structured was siphoned through a simultaneous process and layering of concern with the concern itself. Not only was the shouting addressed as an event, but, at the same time, team members engaged their own interpretations in the service of sorting out what they ostensibly saw and heard with their very own eyes and ears. While, as ethnographers of these data, we more or less know that Jim's behavior will be assigned to a category of either sportsmanship or disturbance, we also take it that the category and structure will be worked out by interpretive laborers.

The concept of structure has a particular tone in practical ethnography, again contrasting with its structural ethnographic counterpart. In the latter, structure can be so highlighted against articulation that ethnographic description virtually collapses structure into the very things and events that structure serves to interpret. As such, structural ethnography produces a native, yet object-like account of field reality in which, as Blumer (1969: 22) once put it, the obdurate experiences of people's native worlds are addressed and "talk back" to us. As Hammersley and Atkinson (1983: chap. 1) suggest, the consequent "naturalism" shortchanges the part that ethnographic orientation itself plays in revealing folk realities. As far as Cedarview's folk world is concerned, structure would be found in the ostensible native meanings of Jim's and others' behaviors, not in their articulation. One would read structure not in the ways that their respective behaviors represented folk reality, but in the native realities their behaviors presented to folk. The difference in emphasis is important, for a naturalistic reading would tend to gloss, if not bothering to record or present in the first place, the articulative processes by which experience was structured into the native realities they were taken to be.

In practical ethnography, structure is representational, but always in relation to concrete particulars, that is, in relation to apparent things and events. In effect, structure is as much a relationship as it is a pattern of experiential realities. If it were not so awkward, we would accurately write structure as the structure-of-this-thing-or-that-event-for-this-or-that-purpose. Practitioners of everyday life use and apply structures and, simultaneously, produce the very realities that concern them. Yet, while simultaneous, they do take different stances toward their actions, evident in turns of their attentions to things and events, on the one side, and to the act of attention in its own right, on the other. The stances converge on concrete concerns in many layers of attention.

Again applying the guiding metaphor, the practical ethnographer encounters a field of folk at work making sense of everyday life. Folk carry with them a developing stock of structures, or interpretive tools, for assigning meaning to their worlds' particulars. In application, the tools shape and give concrete meaning to what they behold. In this regard, it is important to note that the sense of structure in practical ethnography is neither the objective, logical reality it is in continental structuralism (see Kurzweil, 1980), which collapses things and events into concrete experiential systems, nor the objective reality it is in American structuralism (see Blau, 1975; Lemert, 1979), which distills the intelligibility of experience into objective systems of things and events.

Another way to envision the structure engaging the practitioner of everyday life is to think of structure as a kind of tension, an objectivity in the making, achieved yet always subject to questioning and reconsideration. Concrete structure is interpretive time frozen, so to speak (see Giddens, 1979). Referring to our earlier examples, Jim's shouting, like any other incident, is interpretively loaded with potential realities, to be triggered by those dealing with it. To structure the event as emotional disturbance is virtually to freeze it for actual inspection or embellishment as the pathological condition it is. Once so realized, the structure that the shouting becomes both presents its bestowed reality to those concerned and guides their conduct. Yet, as practical structures, they can be interpretively thawed and refrozen, as it were, exemplified by a team member who wonders audibly if the team is perhaps inadvertently labeling Jim's behavior when it actually could be something entirely different from a blowup.

Practical ethnography also contrasts with articulative ethnography in that practical ethnography strikes a greater balance with structure. Mentioned earlier, an ethnographic orientation to articulation, its rules or rule-like processes, cheats us of the concrete form and substance of everyday life. As Van Maanen put it in a personal communication, there is more to interpretation than a rule-book. There are the diversely complex things and events of our worlds, structured according to the varied senses of order folk have available to them, discover, or are responsible for putting into effect. As a practical ethnographer, my own view of what it means to be faithful to the empirical world involves not overshadowing what people take to be real with their attempt to sort it all out. In terms of Figure 1.1, it means not emphasizing the overlap of the top circles at the expense of their separate, yet joint domains. To think of people as everyday philosophers is one thing; to make sophists out of them is quite another.

The sense of structure in articulative ethnography can easily become identified with the structure of articulation itself, the virtual rule-book to which Van Maanen refers. Reality becomes its speaking and communication rules: testimony, conversation, grammar. In our earlier examples, structure would be located in classification rules, layering rules, rules for evaluating rules, and so on. At the extreme, ethnographic accounts cannot even be done, for time would never be frozen into meaningful observables. We run up against the ancient philosophical problem of the state of pure relativism. This is actually shortchanged in Escher's *Drawing Hands,* for the fact that the hands are shown captures a structure: We see hands, not nothing.

My own ethnographic experience has repeatedly shown that to bury experience in articulation is to offer only half a picture. I don't believe Fats Waller was quite right when he made the now famous remark, "One never knows, do one?" It was evident to me, in field after field, that those I've observed did act at times as if they fully and firmly knew what the things and events were that concerned them. But I took it that they had the wits, too, both to confirm and to dislodge what they felt to be real and certain. Their certainties were not merely reality glosses covering a basic flux of experience; they were a very part of the flux.

We have heard Cedarview staff members actually recall, in a team review, the emotional disturbance in a boy's endgame shouting, just as we have heard them challenge the firm belief and its observables. The staff members' engagement with things and events was, as such, never pure articulation, but practical courses of structuring and destructuring (see Gubrium, 1987b). As Garfinkel (1967) himself suggested by way of what ethnomethodologists call "breaching experiments," the collapse of any sense of everyday reality immediately spawns another structuring, another reality, even if the latter is the sum and substance of immediately past attention to things and events. (Indeed, madness itself is not what it implies, for it is recognized only through its communicative structures.) Cedarview staff continually breached their sense of the reality of children's behavior, now attending to its meaning and now turning attention to the quality of their concern in having done so. It was evident that, in practice, the realities of the team's own conduct were not in a category separate from the realities of the children's behavior, although teams and staff members produced endless reports for outside agents that showed little or no trace of the connection.

Considered in the context of experiential time, we find that people inexorably attend to structures, thereby, in time passing, seeing to and through the apparent things and events of concern to them, never being able to collapse it all into the pure experience of articulation. As Derrida (1973, 1978) suggests in the idea of "difference," Cedarview staff members, just as others do, continually defer to the very realities they must create, the meaningful things and events at which they look and think back upon, as they now interpret their worlds. As such, experiential time in practical ethnography is always past (or in a past's future), yet always subject to the interpretive tension of the inquiring but inscrutable present. Articulative ethnography aims toward the latter in its ethnographic orientation. Structural ethnography tends to orient chiefly to the evident past, even, ironically, as many of its ethnographers have been urged to write their monographs in "ethnographic present."

There is ample evidence of concerted interest in the real and reality, even when articulation seems to be at the empirical forefront. Time and again, in the settings studied, I witnessed staff members consider those in their charge for a variety of official reasons, from tallying blowups to assessing mental statuses and felt burdens of care. In the process, it was commonplace for members to turn their attentions from the express things and events of concern to them to the concern itself, even while both were inexorably part of all their actions. They would caution each other to take better care in measurement or evaluation. They would argue over points of view. They would conduct more or less friendly debates over the bases of their agreements and disagreements. As mentioned earlier, they would skillfully, even artfully, attend to their charges and their concerns in layer upon layer of attention to both structure and passing articulation. Who was I to emphasize one or the other as the fundamental domain of their experience?

I witnessed the delimitation of articulative attention. When a disagreement, say, over a point of view in approaching behavior, was extended, it was not uncommon for someone to remind others that they might best, for some reason, turn their attention away from themselves or "unrealistic" conceptual indulgences and back toward their clients, patients, families, children, adolescents, adults, or elders. Thus the delimitation of articulative attention typically was justified in some way; it was worked at, not simply a halting feature of discourse. A common justification was that time was running out in a period formally set aside to structure things and events in some way or other. Another delimitation was objectivistic, where rumination over the meanings of things and events and how to determine them was clipped by what might be called "reality assertions." For example, those deliberating the nosological meaning of emotional disturbance might be reminded that the children being discussed were, after all, emotionally disturbed, not just kids. Or those attempting to distinguish what were normal lapses of memory from pathological forgetfulness in old age might be cautioned that the forgetfulness under consideration was, in any case, a real disease, not just absentmindedness. Indeed, in regard to the latter, the Alzheimer's disease community and movement makes extensive justificatory use of a prominent slogan of its public culture: "Alzheimer's disease is not normal aging!" (Gubrium, 1986a, 1986b). Yet another delimitation ironically cautioned against coming too close to the reflexive articulative whirlwind implicit in Escher's *Drawing Hands*. It was expressed in the assertion that if those concerned continued to be so philosophical about everything, they would simply get nowhere fast. As a doctor once put it, "We can contemplate our navels till kingdom come and we'll never solve this." In such delimitation, it was apparent that, in their own fashion, those concerned took a native accounting of reality in the balance of structure and articulation.

The three delimitations reflect, respectively, three general types of articulative containment, three means by which folk inform each other and us, as ethnographers, that reality for them is concrete and actual, not a mere language game or panorama of discourses. One type is practical, where those concerned are reminded that their everyday philosophical activity is not an analytic abstraction but is conducted in concrete settings with formal and informal rights and responsibilities. The second type is structural, in which the concerned are alerted to the literal fact that concern is about observable and meaningful things and events. The third type is articulative, a rejection of the nihilism of pure, empty time.

The three types reflect a kind of folk usage of the three ethnographic orientations presented in this chapter. As such, they are more than a typology of articulative delimitations. This affinity with the ethnographic orientations brings us around to the fully overlapping area in Figure 1.1, where all the circles intersect. There is a domain of folk interpretation that reflects its sociological counterpart, showing native use of a full range of ethnographic orientations in figuring everyday life. To recognize this is to make explicit the common cultural commentary and criticism that ethnography offers to us. At the same time, in defense of ethnography as privileged description, the recognition both serves as a concerted basis for making visible full cultural ranges of reality and provides for the continual expansion of commentary on experiential horizons.

3. OBSERVING AND DOCUMENTING SOCIAL FORMS

Having discerned and delimited structure and articulation, let us, as people do in practice, turn away from analytic abstractions and consider how to observe and document concrete social forms. We consider three forms of common interest to social scientists and laypersons: personality, role, and family. Data are presented from the field settings studied. In this chapter, the practical structuring and articulation of the forms are highlighted; in the next chapter, the organizational conditioning of the process and forms is emphasized.

Social Forms

Before we begin, a few words about the term *social form,* a common sociological usage. Some would say role is the quintessential social form; others would tout the family. While the choice no doubt has certain political undertones (see Bernardes, forthcoming a), the idea of social form nonetheless refers to a structure we hold in common. Social forms are ways of denoting and organizing everyday life. There is a wealth of forms, well beyond personality, role, and family, extending to the state, community, social class, formal organization, cliques, gangs, and dyads. Together they are the stuff of social life. As Durkheim (1964) emphasized, they are objects in a category by themselves, separate from the things of the inner mind, the body, or even the universe. It was Durkheim's way of making a case for a domain of nature requiring its own method and theory, the subject matter of the social sciences.

Lest we ignore Durkheim's overall project, we should take care not to objectify the term *social form* beyond recognition. As I believe Durkheim (1961) showed in his later work, social form refers as much to a relationship as it does to a thing. Mauss, for example, who was in the same tradition as Durkheim, argued that "person" was a common or public category of the human mind (see Carrithers et al., 1985). It was a habit of those in the Année sociologique school to forge understandings of society by examining the relationship between things and social life, arguing that the shape and substance of social forms grew out of and reflected living.

Taking a lead from Durkheim, I shall treat the social form as both a relationship and a thing. Just as I tried to highlight the practical and constructive quality of things and events in the last chapter by hyphenating their terms of reference, I take personality, role, and family to be both structures of social life and concrete things and events. They are particular things in their own right only in relation to those who attend to them in that way. For example, not only is the family a specific set of social bonds but it is also a way of thinking about, and perceiving, the bonds (see Gubrium and Buckholdt, 1982b; Gubrium and Lynott,

1985b). While we might designate a family by literally pointing to its members or its household, we know that some folk who live in households are not legal families but nonetheless feel and act like families and that some relatives are anything but "family-like." Accordingly, we find that, to be inclusive of the variety of familial applications, we might best decide that some social bonds are legally and biologically assigned family status while other social bonds are assigned family status on other grounds.

Assignment is a relationship between a way of structuring things and events on the one side and things and events on the other. Articulation is the process entailed. This, of course, has been represented in Figure 1.1. Yet, to emphasize the relational status of social forms is to distinguish the potential structurings of each particular aspect of everyday life. In regard to family, it suggests that any event that occurs to, and between, people may be thought of as, and claimed to be, familial, regardless of its legal or biological status. It suggests, too, that any ostensible material token of the same relationship, such as its things (rings, households) and rituals, may be taken to be signs of what the relation is not, of the unfamilial.

The idea of social forms being both relationships and things is another way of drawing attention to structure and articulation. In that respect, we might think of the social form as a kind of structure—social structure. But folk theories, too, are a kind of social structure, as is any configuration for bestowing order to the things and events of everyday life. People inspect, discern, define, and reorder their worlds according to what structures make intelligible. As articulated, structures are not fixed social configurations. Family, for example, is only a candidate structure for any social bond, legally familial or not. In the experiences of those concerned, some formal marriages are anything but nuptial bonds or wedded bliss; some social linkages, while not formally wedded, are like marriages made in heaven. In the variations, it is evident that the experiential and interpretive relationship of those concerned to the social facts of their lives is as definitive of the latter as what the latter inform them of the meaning of their lives in their own rights.

There is an important theoretical point to be gained from this method of thinking about social forms. If we limit the analysis of social forms to the ostensible things and events they define, we have little or no way of taking into account nonstandard forms, such as fictive families, except by thinking of them as deviant, exceptional products of conditions that anomalize what otherwise would be natural, or as signs of larger processes of social change. The point is that the limitation would tend to separate our theoretical understanding of the normal or standard from the so-called abnormal or nonstandard. In contrast, in taking social forms to be both things and relationships, we do not, a priori, analytically foreclose the study of diverse, say, familial forms, as part and parcel of the study of the family. Sociological forms are thus not automatically identified with any particular public or personal preference.

Durkheim had a rather apt way of referring to the relational quality of social forms; he called them "collective representations." Things like society, community, person, and family, while social facts, also represented or signaled collective life. They were an ensemble of social identities that, in their particular applications—such as this or that kind of family—served to present to those concerned, and inform them about, the conditions and configurations of their lives. However, other than tracing parallels between social arrangements and collective representations from one kind of society to another, the Durkheimians provided us with very little method for studying the nature and dynamics of social forms as practical relationships. For that, we turn to articulative ethnography, where social forms are seen in processes of formation and transformation. At the same time, emphasizing practice, we are attuned to the folk realities getting defined or altered in recognizable ways.

Personality

The usual disciplinary divisions might suggest that personality was not a social form, part of psychology, not sociology. Indeed, if we had insisted on orienting ourselves to forms as things, not equally as relationships, it would have made good sense to classify some things social and the rest otherwise. The relational quality of all forms, so-called social as well as others, changes all of that. Like other forms, personality can be thought of as a means of interpreting and, thereby, giving structure to things and events. Ricoeur (1970) took a similar tack in interpreting Freud's "mind."

If we think of personality as a structure, as a way of structuring behavior, and we turn to related folk concerns, we see and hear how personality serves as a practical means for understanding conduct as well as how personality competes with other forms in the process. While personality was a subject of great interest in all the field sites, I'll focus on Wilshire, a physical rehabilitation hospital (Gubrium and Buckholdt, 1982a), where personality, as a usage, was differentially linked with two prevailing images of treatment and recovery.

Patients were admitted to Wilshire for a variety of problems falling broadly within physical medicine. Wilshire was a free-standing, full-service facility. Problems included the physical functions compromised by spinal cord injury, brain trauma, stroke, hip fractures, and amputation. Physical incapacities were treated, not the bodily injuries themselves. Physiatrists were its medical specialists. Rehabilitation services included physical and occupational therapy, speech therapy, and consulting specialists in psychology and psychiatry. At Wilshire, the services were supported by nursing, social work, and combined special modalities such as hydrotherapy, diathermy, and ultrasound. By and large, patients were referred to Wilshire from acute care facilities following an injury or incapacitating surgery. The average length of stay was four to six weeks. Some patients were released to their families and returned to households; others, especially older patients, were transferred to nursing homes for extended care; a few returned to acute care hospitals for the treatment of intercurrent illnesses.

As in any treatment facility, there were many therapeutic strategies and complex apparatuses. I won't dwell on the technical side of treatment and recovery, for it was not strictly there that Wilshire patients, staff members, families, and significant others interpreted the parts they played in recovery. Rather, interpretation was informed by two rather distinct images of rehabilitation contained in the hospital's therapeutic culture: educational and medical conceptions. The technical side of treatment and recovery, together with categories of service and recovery timetables, were mediated likewise.

Before I elaborate on the images as structures of recovery connected with personality as a social form, a few words about the images' method of discovery. I use the term *discovery* because the images were never introduced to me in those terms or as distinct structures, although it was not uncommon to hear references to the "medical model" of rehabilitation as opposed to other approaches. The term *discovery* might be written as "dis-cover," inferring a process of removing the cover—the surface—from something. In general, ethnography is not just another folk interpretation but makes visible the experiential grounds of things and events, what is largely tacit, taken for granted, or treated by people as ancillary to concrete matters of everyday life. In particular, practical ethnography retrieves both concrete matter's structures and articulations in the "deconstruction" of field realities. Accordingly, in the fieldwork, the method was to attempt to discover an underlying principle or set of principles that, when discerned, would shed reasonable light on the diverse yet related things Wilshire folk said about rehabilitation. What they said was diverse indeed, from claiming the medical triumphs of recovering patients to asserting that recovery had little or nothing to do with medical or therapeutic intervention. The method involved a continual ethnographic movement back and forth between the actual statements made by Wilshire folk about the process of recovery, on the one hand, and the descriptive organization of the communications, on the other.

In the course of the study, it became evident that the variety of things said about recovery, some more or less explicitly mentioning model or other ways of thinking, seemed to center on either of two competing senses of what the process of recovery was "all about," as it was sometimes put. In therapy, what was conveyed about recovery in testimony and conversation seemed uniform enough. One physical therapist after another informed patients that patients would not make any progress in rehabilitation unless they put their minds to it. Typically, therapists explained that rehabilitation was a matter of teaching and learning, that the therapists and other staff members could only inform and guide recovery. The therapeutic function was, in that sense, an educational one. It depended critically on the patient's attitude toward learning and his or her effort to put what was taught into practice. Therapists repeatedly reminded patients that the staff could in no way cure their problems and that, if anyone was the doctor, it was the patient. Actually, medical terminology was shunned as staff cautioned patients not to think of being cured, referring to patients as good, average, or poor students and, in turn, encouraging them to think of the therapist as a teacher.

This was not just a therapist's way of speaking about the process of recovery; doctors, too, used the language. At Wilshire, there were support groups for patients with particular types of rehabilitation problems. In the spinal cord injury group, for example, the physiatrist often presented the physiology of paraplegia and quadriplegia. Especially noteworthy were sessions dealing with bowel and bladder control. The physiatrist highlighted the fact that patients would have to take cues from their bodies in order to adapt to paralysis. Cure was rarely part of the lesson, as learning and motivation were highlighted and the need to listen attentively and develop good habits encouraged. Doctors also supported the educational efforts of therapists by conveying the need for hard work and self-reliance, confirming what patients repeatedly heard in their therapy sessions.

When I asked the therapists about the meaning of recovery, their answers were more diverse. On the one hand, I was told about teaching and learning, the need to motivate the patient, and the importance of good teaching skills. The comments coincided with what the working patient was said to be "actually" doing in the process of recovery and how therapists and other staff entered into it. On the other hand, I also was told that patients could remain inpatients only if they were benefiting from therapy, from treatment designed to effect reasonable progress toward rehabilitation. In this vein, I was reminded time and again, especially by the utilization review coordinator, that if staff could not show effective medical treatment and the resulting patient progress, the patient had to be discharged. From these comments, I began to suspect that recovery could be something quite different from what was implied, if not outright claimed, in the context of staff relations with the working patient. In particular, I heard more references to treatment and cure, less to teaching and learning. At times, especially in utilization review conferences, there were express suggestions of the need to show treatment progress, if there were not explicit directives to do so. The need meant the requirement of documenting for third-party payers the success of therapeutic intervention as evidence of normal progress toward recovery. What was being said overlaid an entirely different sense of rehabilitation than I had otherwise encountered and presumed—a medical therapeutic function.

In the varied communications about the process of recovery, I was discovering two rehabilitation structures, which, at the time, I called rehabilitation "images." Just as the colloquial expression that one "knows where someone is coming from" serves to convey knowledge of an underlying principle that makes a person's conduct meaningful, I had located two structures that informed and patterned staff articulations of the process of recovery. It is important to note that it was only when I discovered and heard the contrast between educational and medical references that the idea of underlying images occurred to me in the first place. The images informed me "where staff were coming from," as they now spoke one thing and now spoke quite another with equal conviction and sophistication concerning what "rehabilitation is all about." Before that, the variety of expressions seemed more anomalous and arbitrary than socially patterned, more about contradictions than relationships.

In terms of the images, the cones stacked by patients in occupational therapy could mean that what was really taking place was either the patient learning, on the one hand, or the successful application of therapeutic skills, on the other. In an educational frame, every bit and piece of the recovery experience (including its things, such as therapeutic apparatus, prosthetic and orthotic appliances, and range-of-motion exercises, and its events, such as progress and physical assessment) were articulated in relation to teaching and learning. To use Weber's expression again, staff attached educational meaning as they figured patients' and staff's related behaviors. In a medical framing, the "same" bits and pieces assembled the realities of therapeutic intervention and doctoring.

Yet, articulation was not simply a matter of skillfully designating and assigning educational or medical meaning to rehabilitation. Audience was an important practical component of the process. Therapeutic staff communicated with three important audiences at Wilshire: patients, patients' families, and third-party payers. Communication with patients about the process of recovery was structured by the educational image. As mentioned earlier, patients were routinely reminded that they needed to learn in order to make progress, that no one was about to cure them. In contrast, communications with third-party payers were structured in medical terms, never denying that what staff members were doing was, after all, skilled intervention, even though, in utilization reviews, there was unreported talk about patient motivation and attitude in considering "how to put it" for reporting purposes. With patients' families, the structure articulated depended significantly on how successful rehabilitation was said to be, a medical structuring tending to frame successes and an educational one informing the language and communication of failure.

It was in relation to the audience variations that personality emerged as both an important social form and a message. In describing successful rehabilitation to families and in the utilization reviews required by hospital regulations, the patient's personality took a distinct back seat to the language of treatment. Communicatively highlighted was whatever had been done to effect progress, on the one hand, and assessments of ensuing progress, on the other. There also were discussions of what could be expected from continued treatment and estimates of when maximum benefit would be achieved.

When the audience was the working patient, as in therapy and educational sessions, personality came to the fore. In these situations, it was commonplace to hear staff speak of the difference motivation can make in recovery. It was not unusual for therapists to directly caution patients that some persons never made it in rehabilitation because of their overall attitude or the kind of person they were. Indeed, there were times when therapists pointed out that in rehabilitation, personality, if not motivation and attitude, was everything, that the right person could work wonders in recovery and the wrong one get nowhere, notwithstanding staff efforts and the elaborate treatment technology.

Personality was also a significant reality in the communication of poor progress to families. When therapists had done all they could for a patient, personality was used to explain why progress had not been made when there was reason to expect it could have been achieved in such cases. As in staff's communication with the working patient, the person was separated from the patient, the former treated as an explanation for the latter's apparent lack of success. While families were informed of the technical details of limited recovery, they also were told of the need for a positive attitude to make significant progress. In turn, family members addressed the patient's personality in their own terms, agreeing or disagreeing with staff assessments, but, nonetheless, taking the social form into account in their responses in a way it was not considered in exchanges about successful rehabilitation.

Adapting Durkheim's usage, personality was a collective representation because its communicative reality reflected what those concerned were doing with words. To explain that progress in rehabilitation was entirely the result of the patient's personality, especially motivation, signaled a relationship and structure, just as to explain that progress stemmed from intervention and treatment signaled another relationship and structure. According to circumstance, bits and pieces of the patient's person were salvaged for different purposes. At the same time, personality served to make intelligible its related concrete things and events.

While considerations of personality are often relegated to psychology, it was evident at Wilshire and in the other field settings studied that personality was a social form. It was an important *thing* addressed, sorted, and communicated in attending to the everyday realities of rehabilitation. Personality was a shared entity, denotable in concrete facets of relevant experiences, even while its precise significance could vary and its evidence be debated. Yet, personality was a thing used, not just an object, again signaling its collective representation.

Role

In contrast to personality, role is a favored point of departure for sociologists. Some give it a behavioral twist, seeing roles in patterns of interrelated conduct; others emphasize the normative side, where role is taken to be the expectation that behavior follows a certain pattern. Whatever the emphasis, role is more or less a thing, a social form that tells of regular linkages between people. Some familiar roles, of course, are mother, father, student, leader, boss, and patient. Each can be seen as a behavior in that it informs us of its occupant's activity; each also can be taken as an anticipation in that it signals what anyone occupying it is more or less expected to do.

Role is a quintessential social entity. Each role is also what it is not, as we might denote in saying that a mother is not a father, a boss is not an employee, a student not a teacher, a patient not a doctor, and so on. Role takes on its meaning in the linkages it has with other roles, bound together in the diverse social scenes we call society. Being a social form, role is in a category by itself, not reducible to the individual character- istics of the player or to the personality that fills it. Its logic stems more from linkages than occupants, though occupants certainly play a part, so to speak.

In observing and documenting roles and their relationships, we might do as Whyte (1955) did in his Cornerville study and find that regardless of the athletic skills of individual corner boys, their competitiveness, successes, and failures were attuned to the roles they played in relationship to each other. They played less well as followers than as leaders in ostensible games of equals. Roles were a source of behavior regulation separate from individual traits and abilities.

If we take a closer look at the folk practices engaged in articulating roles, we see that, as available social forms, roles also are ways used to structure conduct. The emphasis stresses a different sense of relation- ship, recalling our earlier definition of social forms as relationships as well as things. Not only are roles social objects because of their relationship with other social objects (for example, as patient to doctor), but roles are social things, too, in relation to what those concerned do with them.

Referring to the terminology of Figure 1.1, we can think of role as an available structure for assigning meaning to the things and events of everyday life. It is important to note that, in this sense of relationship, role relates to people not just as a guide for action, but also as a resource for assigning meaning and thereby lending order to social linkages. As such, roles do not operate behind their players' backs, organizing players' conduct in relationship to each other, but more or less serve the practical everyday purposes of those concerned in dealing with related affairs.

To speak of a role as a structure or usage, of course, suggests that there are other structures or usages, such as the use of personality to interpret recovery in rehabilitation. We heard the language of motivation and achievement spoken with the working patient, not the language of medical relations. While the therapist, of course, framed a concern with motivation and achievement in terms of the student-teacher role, the latter was taken to be a way of discerning the exclusive reality of individual motivation in the process of recovery, not a way of claiming that the therapist was actually a teacher, even though the metaphor at times was all too real.

If we think of role as an interpretive structure, those who use it present us with yet another means of understanding their lives. People themselves, not just sociologists, use the familiar sociological lingo in assembling the meaning of their affairs. Combining this with personality as a social form and putting it in disciplinary terms, we encounter people with the conceptual units for assembling everyday life in either personal or social terms. If we permit ourselves, as ethnographers, to hear the diverse and varied disciplinary languages in use that people speak, we again come into touch with the mundane, yet eloquent, everyday philosophers they are. Needless to say, we risk learning, too, that disciplines defined rigidly in terms of specific structures stand to be parochial, if not culturally apologetic, endeavors.

With the idea that role is as much a social formation as a social form, what do we observe and document in situations where those concerned charge themselves with the task of discovering the meaning of their own lives? While, in some sense, as Figure 1.1 presents the folk philosophy of everyday life, all situations are encounters with the question, some situations literally announce it. This was the case in the study of support groups for the caregivers of Alzheimer's disease patients (Gubrium, 1986a, 1986b, 1987; Gubrium and Lynott, 1985a).

Alzheimer's disease (senile dementia) is an incurable, progressive deterioration of mental functioning causing victims to become confused, forgetful, disoriented, and depressed (Reisberg, 1981). Some say it occurs in stages, where initial forgetfulness and intermittent confusion eventually lead to a vegetative existence in which one is incapable of completing the simplest tasks (Hayter, 1974; Bartol, 1979). Others question the developmental logic but, nonetheless, describe gradual loss of function (see Gubrium, 1986a). Because Alzheimer's is a progressive dementia that, in time, poses a tremendous care burden, a major theme of the disease experience is the so-called "second victim," the travail of the caregiver.

Founded in 1979, the Alzheimer's Disease and Related Disorders Association (ADRDA) is a national network of local chapters and support groups, one goal of which is to aid, educate, and counsel family members, and to provide caregivers with forums for mutual support (Alzheimer's Disease and Related Disorders Association, 1982). Support groups for caregivers were observed in two cities. The participants were victims' spouses, adult children, siblings, and significant others. In sharing their caregiving experiences, participants continually confronted the task of interpreting the meanings of their relationships with the victim as part of attempting to understand personal and familial responsibilities. The concern was far from being a mere exercise in self-examination, for interpretations helped to define where and how the victims' care would be organized and when that would change. Accordingly, another major theme was the question of when "it's time," a familiar expression referring to when it's time to curtail home care and seek an institutional placement, usually a nursing home.

In the support groups, caregivers learned that being responsible for the victim could present a virtual "36-hour day" burden, another common expression (Mace and Rabins, 1981). Participation sensitized caregivers to a growing public culture of questions and answers about the disease experience (see Gubrium, 1986: chap. 4). The public culture was found in the many ADRDA chapter and national newsletters, in television programming and public service announcements, in films and videotapes depicting the disease and its diverse yet common caregiving experiences, in support group and local chapter folklore, in the "how-to" books for caregivers and family members, in the professional and semiprofessional disease literature, and in public interest documents. Some participants limited their quests for answers to local chapter folklore and how-to books; others avidly read the disease's professional literature.

The support groups were an encounter between individuals pressed by a concern with the meaning of the disease experience, on one side, and by a growing stock of resources (roles among them) for structuring the experience, on the other. Ethnographic interest was centered on how the two were bridged, how bits and pieces of the disease experience became something recognized and shared and, in turn, how what was ostensibly held in common represented the particulars. It was a version of the connection Mills (1959, 1963) had formulated between public issues and private troubles, except that I was documenting the link in decidedly face-to-face encounters.

My theory was as much method as the usual observing, writing, and reporting tools of the trade. As a practical brand of ethnography suggested, I was not just to observe roles, relationships, group structures, and personalities, but the ways those concerned used the forms to understand their own and the victims' lives. The difference in emphasis affected what was actually observed as field realities and, of course, what was documented. As a practical ethnography also suggested, an endless process of interpretive usage was not to be observed, but a process that, time and again, settled and unsettled its affairs with the questions fueling it. In other words, I aimed to inspect and analyze structure and articulation as two—interpenetrating—sides of field reality.

As an example, take Vera Pastor's experience. She was the 68-year-old caregiver of David, her 73-year-old demented husband. Typically, Vera had at first refused to believe that anything was wrong with David. He occasionally forgot to come home from the dry goods store he owned. To Vera, this meant that he was just getting forgetful, something she knew happened with age. She had found over the years that her own memory was not what it had been. After David had a mild heart attack, Vera noticed that his memory worsened markedly. He lost his way around the neighborhood. He no longer had an aptitude for figures and the family business had to be sold. Meanwhile, Vera learned that David had Alzheimer's disease and was told by his doctor that she might best start thinking about a nursing home.

Vera described all of this and more at the first meeting of an ADRDA support group she attended. She had come into contact with the organization after calling a telephone number given in a television public service ad. She was not the only one to tell her story in that support group session. A facilitator, who had been a caregiver herself, encouraged all newcomers to introduce themselves and describe their caregiving situation. Veteran participants, too, spoke of their experiences. All presented in turn, listened, compared, and contrasted.

While Vera came to the support group with some understanding of Alzheimer's disease obtained from the popular magazine articles she had read as well as from what her doctor and a few friends had told her, she spoke often at that first meeting of not knowing what would happen to her own husband and, with equal concern, about what was happening to herself as she saw him decline and the burdens of care became overwhelming. Vera's testimony, like others', was not a mere litany of daily travail. It also came from the heart and conveyed the personal hurt of tenuous love, the determination to keep devotion alive, the embarrassment of bizarre conduct, and an oscillating rage at the insidious effects of the disease. As Vera recalled in despair:

> I asked God what is happening to my David. I don't know. David can't tell me anymore. He sometimes doesn't even know it's me, Vera. And I ask myself, too, what's happening to me? Excuse me please for saying, but I sometimes wonder if I can still be Vera [weeps].

Vera's was one of many stories of personal quandary. Some, like Vera, focused on both physical and personal burdens and their related questions. Others dwelled on how to deal with the victim's growing physical needs; theirs were virtually selfless depictions. Still others were primarily soul-wrenching attempts to reach out for help in dealing with mixed emotions rooted in shaken attachments and competing allegiances.

Participants met the challenge of sorting out feelings, concerns, and travails. At the same time, the "support" formed and shaped the many questions asked and answers provided. Participants' exchanges showed evidence of two major ways of structuring personal quandary, one based in personality and the other in roles, part of the disease's public culture. While the concepts of personality and role are building blocks of psychology and sociology, it was clear that participants themselves constructed experiential understandings with the same resources. Comments and conversation showed that what became known of themselves as individuals and the ways they did or did not resemble each other was not a simple by-product of the persons they were, the roles they took in caregiving, or related experiential trajectories (see Goffman, 1961; Glaser and Strauss, 1968). Rather, the knowledge was mediated by the persons, roles, and timelines they assigned to each other, as explanations for their own and the victim's inner experiences (see Gubrium and Buckholdt, 1977).

When Vera, for example, blurted out at one point, in self-disgust, "What kind of person wonders if she still loves her husband of 40 years?" another participant immediately responded:

I'd say it was something that each and every one of us goes through in this thing; what you just go through. It's too bad, but it's not you, ya know. I wouldn't blame myself for it.

The comment and response ethnographically signaled both structure and articulation. As far as structure was concerned, the statements suggested that what was happening to Vera could be either a product of the kind of person she was or what any kind of person in her situation would experience. When another participant who directed her comment to Vera repeated that Vera could hardly blame herself for her emotions, that Vera was just "playing out" what was natural, and, unfortunately, was at a "stage in the thing" when anyone is at her lowest, the participant elaborated the implicit career of the caregiving role. It was presented as a normal and commonplace series of changing identities, reflecting a well-known means of interpreting the "second victim's" experience over time.

As it happened time and again in the support groups, it was soon evident in talk that participants were not just sharing feelings, but shaping and forming—articulating—their feelings' interpretive context out of prevailing understandings. Vera could be one who had personally failed at the deepest level of filial responsibility and to be blamed for it, or she could be one who had taken the role of caregiver, was experiencing its normal course of development, and was not to be accused for what was happening. Ongoing testimony showed that person and role were continuously available options for structuring emotional experience (see Lynott, 1983), not to be likened to a conversion experience. The structuring of emotional experience had an open horizon of choices for how individuals could judge themselves as family members, such as whether to blame themselves for what was happening or to accept it reluctantly as a normal part of the course of events.

On occasion, person and role came into considerable competition. Some participants refused to accept the normal-course-of-events approach and insisted on seeing what was happening to themselves in terms of their unique responses. As one of them asked and commented in irritation:

How can you tell me it's normal? I know what I'm feeling like no one else, and I know better than anyone here what's happening to him [her demented husband] deep down. Sure I blame myself for having the nagging doubts because, well, I just shouldn't have them, that's all! And don't tell me I'm denying either. Each person is unique. Let's not forget that.

Others claimed the very opposite, challenging the unique-personal-response approach with recognizable affective roles for the interpretation of emotional experience.

Support group proceedings showed that the experiential reality of caregiving, particularly its emotional underlife, was a relationship as much as it was a thing. The support group and its interpretive culture provided participants a distinct configuration of optional experiential realities, mediated by their articulation. Caregivers who came to see their inner experiences in terms of the normal-course-of-events approach discovered that their inner feelings weren't unique but a particular instance of something larger and impersonal. It was informed by an available structure: the theme and role of the responding caregiver. Those who continued to interpret themselves as uniquely experiencing the disease's travails learned the concrete thing they were in relation to a different understanding, one grounded in personality, privacy, and self-blame. In this sense, role (as well as person) was as much a way of thinking about pattern and expectation in human experience as it was an object of experience.

Family

Finally, let us turn to family as a social form. Like person and role, we commonly think of the family as a thing, as a set of social relationships defined by biological, quasibiological, or legal ties. It is the thing writ large we are as networks of mothers, fathers, grandparents, children, and extended kindred. Of course, we don't actually hear or see the abstract family in the large, only its members. Indeed, members themselves do not directly see and hear the family they are, only their representations of who they are as kindred in the large (see Gubrium and Lynott, 1985b). The same point could have been made in regard to personality and role. While we commonly think of them as things or entities, what we see and hear when, say, the person behaves and speaks is not actually a personality but a moving body and a voice. The fact that we can intelligibly ask what the motions and verbalization mean attests to the distinction. Likewise, while sociologists take role to be a building block of society, a social entity par excellence, they don't actually see social relationships, only contacts. As such, the practical question of who speaks for the social forms becomes significant (see Gubrium, 1986b).

Thorne, Yalom, and others (1982) and Bernardes (1984, 1985, forthcoming a, forthcoming b) have suggested that to even pose empirical questions in terms of "THE family" forecloses the investigation of familial representation and interpretation. The question of who speaks for the family is, analytically and ethnographically, at considerable odds with concern over the organization and composition of the family as an entity. I believe that this is another way of saying that family, as a social form, is as much a social relationship as it is a thing.

Following this and related work (Gubrium and Lynott, 1985b; Gubrium, 1987a; Gubrium and Holstein, 1987; Gubrium, forthcoming), let us consider how we might observe and document family as a way of thinking about, and articulating, human relationships. Each field setting studied showed evidence of family usage. In the nursing home, patient care conference participants variously used what they knew of the family life of patients to set short- and long-range goals (Gubrium, 1975). Cedarview staff saw the family as a major ingredient in childhood experience and selectively used it to explain emotional disturbance (Buckholdt and Gubrium, 1985 [1979]). Wilshire staff took families into account in making a variety of treatment and care decisions, especially in discharge planning (Gubrium and Buckholdt, 1982a). The members of the chapters and support groups of the Alzheimer's Disease and Related Disorders Association assumed that family composition and familial responsibility in caregiving were crucial factors in understanding the disease experience and applied their knowledge accordingly.

Family usages were continually mediated by deliberations over the practical question of who speaks for the family. This was not a simple matter of seeking the head of the household or its most articulate member. It was evident that family membership, for example, was only one claim, not *the* claim, for privileged access to familial knowledge Gubrium and Holstein, 1987). As I shall illustrate shortly, the family as a social form could not be separated from the practical matter of how to represent it, which signaled its relationship to structure and articulation.

Take the family caregivers who participated in the Alzheimer's disease support groups. While they conveyed their stories, as Vera Pastor and others did in the last section, it was by no means clear that caregivers' testimony was taken implicitly to present the truest picture of domestic life. For example, when Martha Infeld, on one occasion, spoke of all that she, her daughter, and her son had done every day for her rapidly declining husband, to keep him, as Martha put it, "in his own home and at the highest level of functioning possible," another caregiver, Harvey, asked if Martha wasn't perhaps doing too much. The testimony and question ethnographically suggested the possibility of two different ways to interpret the household matters Martha described. Was it possible that—no matter what was said to characterize family life and no matter what was described as being done for the patient—the meaning of domestic life regarding caregiving was a relationship in the same way we considered other social forms to be both objects and relationships?

Before we reach too hasty a conclusion, consider what was heard and observed as deliberation over Martha's testimony unfolded. Martha responded that she was not sure what Harvey meant, that as far as she could see, she and her two children were doing all that could be done. Martha, in fact, became annoyed at a later implication that she was acting out of guilt in caring for her husband, remarking:

I kind of resent what you seem to be saying, Harv. I love my husband and you couldn't ask for more devoted kids. Jan [son] and Minnie [daughter] do things for their father that no one could complain about. We're not doing it because we feel we have to, you know. We're doing what we do for Tom [husband] because the family really cares.

Harvey immediately explained that he hadn't meant anything malicious, only that sometimes what seemed to be total family care and devotion was not filial responsibility at all but a kind of insidious irresponsibility. Harvey pointed out that being responsible in Alzheimer's disease ultimately meant caring enough to realize when "it's time" to consider institutionalization, for the sake of the family as a whole. This led to a rather heated exchange over the meaning of total family care and devotion, centering on the question of whether someone who cared as much as the Infeld family did was really "being family."

The issue of who best speaks for the family was raised and deliberated in conjunction with the question of the true meaning of family responsibility. The issue was evident in Martha's assertions that she knew best what went on in her own home and family because she was there to see it all. It was evident, too, in both Harvey's and other participants' contrary suggestions that Martha might not be seeing things as clearly as an outsider would because she was naturally biased in the matter. Indeed, one participant added that they all had seen and heard many instances of "denial" in times of family crisis. As in Martha's case, the daily burden and headlong devotion combined to color what was really going on, namely, the denial that it might be best at a certain point for all concerned, for both the patient and family members, to consider institutional placement.

At one point, the facilitator, who was a caregiver herself, intervened and asked no one in particular if it wasn't possible that what one might see as filial responsibility, another might interpret as irresponsible? The question launched a series of exchanges focusing on the meaning of family responsibility, in particular what it meant to be family in caring for an Alzheimer's disease victim. What ethnographically emerged in this support group session and was repeatedly observed and documented in others was the existence of two structures for articulating what it meant to be family. One served to interpret bits and pieces of a family's caregiving experience in terms of how much could be done for the victim. Structured in this way, domestic affairs were taken to be more or less evidence of familial devotion, varied degrees of being and doing what was expected of a family. Another structure organized the caregiving experience in terms of what to do in the best interest of the family as a whole, including the victim. In this framework, a demented victim typically was said not to know, anyway, what was being done for him or her. Or, if the victim were aware, it was explained that, in any case, he or she would think it best for all concerned that the family seriously consider "it's time."

No one was simply assumed to have privileged access to domestic life, not even family members. Being a member was only one basis for claiming privileged access; others were outside objectivity, professional experience, and expertise. Indeed, it was not uncommon in the support groups for family members themselves to ask outsiders, more or less acquainted with their familial affairs, to shed light on domestic reality. On several occasions, Martha Infeld herself entertained the possibility that what she and her children were doing as a family might in fact have a different meaning. As such, the many voices and claims of family testimony indicated that family was both a thing and a relationship between the entity as a social form and those who articulated it as one thing or another by means of available structures. While diverse voices were considered a normal therapeutic component of the support group experience in particular, the articulation and structures entailed reflected folk interpretation in general.

It should be noted that, for Martha and others, what the facts showed her family to be—actually responsible or unwittingly irresponsible—was articulated in terms of available structures. The public culture of the Alzheimer's disease movement and the ADRDA, together with each support group's developing caregiving folklore, served as interpretive resources for assigning meaning to individual family troubles, what it meant to "be family." A recurring theme was the responsible family, structured either as totally devoted or as denying broader domestic obligations. As Mills (1959, 1963) might have put it, the family as an interpersonal entity obtained a biography (or reality) against public possibilities. At the same time, the categories for interpreting experience provided by the disease's public culture were select ones, which, with effective application, articulated recognizable but delimited domestic facts. The point is that other contexts, making other structures available, would realize different domestic orders, again according to their varied claimants, a theme taken up in the next chapter.

4. ORGANIZATIONAL EMBEDDEDNESS

The idea of available structures is a point of departure for considering the place of organizational embeddedness in folk interpretation (see Gubrium, 1987a). The term *embeddedness* refers to the practical domain of the articulation and structures making up interpretation. Interpretation does not occur out of time and place, but is engaged within discernibly organized circumstances. For example, while the emotionally disturbed boys we met at the start skillfully disputed claims about ladyfingers, and staff members artfully layered their own understandings on top of that, we found, too, that what the boys' behavior risked becoming depended on the circumstances in which it was considered. We saw that in formal treatment reviews, what was seen benignly on other occasions was likely to be interpreted in accordance with a health/illness categorization. It was not that in formal treatment reviews the boys' behavior was automatically defined as disturbed, but that it risked being conceived as more or less disturbed, not just more or less wily or spirited.

Interpretive Control

What organizational embeddedness stresses is the circumstantial limits of usage. A named organization—like Cedarview or Wilshire—

provides a recognizable means of responding to auspices or taking aegis into account in sorting through the available structures for assigning meaning to things and events, some of which are official and others not. Embeddedness does not mean, of course, that those concerned will necessarily attend to formal auspices, only that they can call each other to task for having, or not having, done so. The possibility and likelihood provide a kind of localized interpretive control, used by those concerned in articulating the particular sense of things.

The ethnographic consideration of filial responsibility in caregiving was not only sensitive to the ways support group participants learned to see and define feelings, but was oriented to circumstance as well. When Martha Infeld, like others, entered her support group, she encountered a new set of categories for interpreting her family's caregiving experience. While she was free to decide whether she would define the experience accordingly, her participation nonetheless presented the challenge of new interpretive structures. Martha was obliged either to deny or to accept them as more or less appropriate. Circumstantially, in the support group, available usage extended to the new possibility that too much caregiving was filially irresponsible. Many comments made by support group participants suggested that usage was organizationally circumscribed. It was not unusual for participants to speak of how they had altered (or should alter) their way of thinking about feelings and care after hearing others describe their experiences, and of how the support group and the ADRDA helped in managing what they had come to know. Of course, not all participants took what they discovered to heart. Those who did not, nonetheless, learned what they did believe by now discovering what they could not abide.

In each of the field sites, people took into account the interpretive agendas of circumstance in discerning the meaning of their experiences. When this broke down, they were routinely reminded of the business at hand or, less formally, of what was taken for granted as a way of seeing things in the circumstance. It was part of the everyday work of managing the interpretive spillovers discussed earlier. The challenges, responses, and discursive control ethnographically signaled organizational embeddedness.

Before we move on, it would be useful, as a point of reference, to graphically illustrate the place of organizational embeddedness in folk interpretation. Figure 4.1 shows some of the relevant detail, expanding on the top circles of Figure 1.1. As the intersecting circles of Figure 4.1 suggest, what is or is not an available reality in any given place like

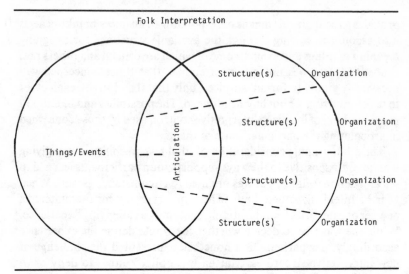

Figure 4.1: Organizational Embeddedness

Cedarview is not a simple matter of structuring things and events along official or formal lines, for articulation itself is subject to articulation.

In the very midst of a formal psychiatric review at Cedarview, it was not uncommon for participants to momentarily recast their considerations of a child's behavior in terms completely separate from whether or not it was disturbed. On one occasion, for example, staffers were presenting details of a child's pica, which is an abnormal craving for inedibles. Pica had led the child to chew on pencils and swallow erasers, among other classroom and cottage paraphernalia. The behavior was despaired and plans laid for putting the child on a program to modify it. At one point, though, when a participant mentioned that the child eats absolutely every crumb of food on her plate, another staffer interjected in jest that she eats the plate, too. This sparked a chain of laughter and humorous embellishments of the plate-eating, the kind of camaraderie observed in similar circumstances in each of the sites studied. For the time being, the child's eating behaviors were not so much symptoms of pica, as they were a source of one-upmanship about the very funny things that kids, especially the most eccentric of them, might do. This was soon set aside when a participant suggested that the review needed to be completed and that they really had to get back to business. As such, the child's eating behavior was reassigned to the category of pica, an "official" restructuring and delimitation of its reality.

Organizationally available structures are not necessarily official. A particular classroom may have specific traditions of its own, just as an organization has a culture broader than its charter. A formal organization, such as Cedarview, might be officially committed to behavioral principles and behavior modification programming, yet accept the services, and engage the discourse, of a psychoanalytically oriented psychiatrist. The official and unofficial, acceptable and unacceptable, cut across each other in complex ways in organizations, available realities being sorted for one practical purpose or another, only some of which may be cast as official or authoritative (see Geertz, 1973; Frost et al., 1985). As such, interpretive control is more rhetorical than it is sheerly authoritative or forceful (see Gubrium et al., 1982; Gubrium and Lynott, 1985b).

There is overlap in available realities between organizations, of course, such as the unofficial ways of thinking about things and events cutting across a society. The demarcated sectors of the right circle in Figure 4.1 perhaps overstress the uniqueness of each organization's structures, presenting them as separate cultures. For that reason, I have chosen to distinguish their respective stocks of interpretive structures with broken lines. Still, the presentational constraints of graphic illustration make it difficult to convey the emergence, transformation, and coalescence of structures and auspices in practical processes of articulation and control. I will attempt to remedy this with descriptions of the organizational conditioning of available realities.

Organizational Embeddedness
and Experiential Location

Social forms have their presumed experiential locations, places believed to present their ultimate realities. For example, while we consider domestic relations in diverse places, from the household to the office, it is commonly taken for granted that, in the final analysis, the familial experience is to be found in the home. Household is the location of last resort when it comes to searching for an answer to the question of what "really" goes on in family life (see Gubrium and Holstein, 1987). While an employee might explain that his or her work is not up to its usual standard because of current domestic troubles, we assume that a careful inspection of the home would shed light on the validity of the claim.

The presumed experiential location of other social forms is likewise culturally specified. While a personality may be assessed by means of others' testimony, it is assumed that it is the individual under consideration who, consciously or unconsciously, holds the ultimate truths of his or her life. The character of roles, too, such as motherhood and being a caregiver, suggests that they are most validly revealed in and about their performances, not in places wholly removed, such as where role performances are discussed or planned. Even the material traces of the state as a social form compel us to seek its most telling truths on or about the premises of governmental, administrative, or diplomatic operations. While national and international propaganda, even disinformation, are thought to affect what we know about state activity, the terms *propaganda* and *disinformation* signal the potential invalidity of not attending to what actually occurs on state premises.

The scientific tenet of objective inspection itself is founded on the assumption that social forms are geographically situated. Henry (1971, 1985 [1965]), for one, chose to study the families of psychotic children by living in their households in order to observe at first hand what the families were actually like. Henry understandably worried over the effect of the obtrusiveness on the validity of his findings, but, at the same time, touted the greater objectivity of observations stemming from the perspective of a disinterested party to family affairs, yet directly focused on domestic observables. In choosing to place himself inside the household to inspect what the families were like and not limiting his research to reports of domestic matters, the experiential location assumption overrode its methodological disadvantages. In her book *Family and Social Network,* Bott (1957) claims on the very first page that the home is the family's "natural habitat," thus justifying her household interviews and observations. Indeed, studies of so-called family myths and fictions rely on the idea that the experiential location assumption can be deceptive while still valid. Those whose household residence seems to imply privileged access to domestic truths—family members—may be duped or blinded to its realities (see Perlmutter and Sauer, forthcoming; Ferreira, 1963; Anderson and Bagarozzi, 1983; Bagarozzi and Anderson, 1982; Jackson, 1973; Laing and Esterson, 1964).

Careful attention to the folk interpretation of social forms suggests that experiential location has a different "logical geography" (Ryle, 1949). Experiential location is not only an assumption of everyday life but is itself diversely articulated. In practice, people consider the assumption's theoretical status at the very same time they attempt to locate and sort experiential truths. The organizations that embed their considerations transform experiential location from a resource for discerning the validity of things and events to a condition of interpretation itself.

In considering the ethnography of experiential location, let us focus on the family as a social form and return to the home care of Alzheimer's disease victims. In family caregivers' support groups, we can actually hear participants theorize the experiential location assumption. For example, it was not uncommon for a caregiver to speak in detail of what family life is really like caring for the victim at home, only to ask, or be asked, whether what was conveyed was "actually" going on. Typically, such questions simultaneously generated discussions of the validity of the privileged access assumed to characterize household membership.

The question of the family's experiential location could be addressed at several levels, layering its articulation. For example, in a support group, Betty Collins, the 59-year-old adult daughter of Phyllis, an 81-year-old Alzheimer's victim, described her mother's incessant night wandering and seemingly endless urge to fold things. Betty explained that the need to be constantly vigilant for Phyllis's whereabouts had brought the whole family together to help monitor the victim. Betty explained that the burden of care had gotten to the point where everyone at home accepted the fact that each would have one sleepless night per week in taking a turn being sentry. Despite the increasing burden of care, Betty emphasized that caregiving had helped the family as a whole. There were tensions, of course, but underlying that there was said to be real family strength.

Ethnographically, we hear Betty conveying events that, according to her, represent a strong family. The serial monitoring and acceptance of a weekly sleepless night were two markers. What Betty saw at home was not the actual family strength she described, but signs of it, the things and events assigned the domestic truth she reported (see Gubrium and Lynott, 1985b).

In a related discussion in Betty's support group, it was recommended that Betty might not so readily dismiss the tensions, that she might actually be overestimating her family's solidarity. One participant, Richard Mansfield, the 73-year-old caregiver of a demented spouse, commented that he had heard the same family characterization by a friend of his, whose mother had Alzheimer's. The family did not turn out to be strong at all, but one at the end of its rope, so to speak, virtually taking its last breath by trying to pitch in equally. While Betty did not alter her initial interpretation, it was clear in her reactions to the comment that she began to pay more critical attention to the tensions she had mentioned. In fact, at one point, Betty asked if others thought the family's monitoring was less filial responsibility than resentful obligation. She added that she had felt all were pitching in because they were "family," in particular, because they loved each other.

The discussion showed evidence of articulative layering as participants successively commented on how to interpret what Betty described. One claimed to "know about these things" because he had seen them many times over, warranting his interpretation on the basis of how broad his observations had been. Another participant claimed to know because she, herself, "had been there," as Betty, too, asserted on one occasion. At one particularly frustrating point of the proceedings, when Betty remarked that no one knew her family as well as she did because none had even stepped into her home, she reproduced in her own way the privileged access assumption of family's ostensible experiential location, implying that the actual family was located in the home, not in its outside detractors' representations. It was evident that the various layers and structures of interpretation were no one's particular mandate.

What perhaps was most telling, ethnographically, about the participants' exchanges was their contention with the locational assumption itself. At one point, after a particularly tender and heartrending discussion of disintegrating families, Richard quietly explained, "So you can see how things can fall apart under your very own nose. We can be so blind to what we think we know better than anyone else." When another participant added that "you start to see things in a different way here [in the support group] and that's what a support group is all about," there was an implicit challenge to the idea that the social order of the family is ultimately located in the household. Indeed, it was not uncommon for participants to actually report that, for better or worse, they saw things and events more clearly in their support group than at home. At times, too, there were also differences of opinion about the matter. It was evident that the location that best represented domestic affairs was not exclusively a matter of method or validity, but also a matter of theorizing about method itself.

To hear those concerned speak of how they thought or felt about things or events "here" or "there"—words that the caregivers and others actually used in reference to their households, their support groups, and other locations—was to learn, once again, that social forms are not just things but relationships. The logical geography of social forms was not just a cultural presumption about their placement but a practical artifact of organizational embeddedness.

In regard to the family, what really goes on at home was not only a matter of facts, but the available realities of structures differentially distributed in organized social life. Caregiver support groups, for example, were organizations that, in embedding the articulation of the family in their particular discursive conventions, served to structure and realize family as a thing in ways it was not likely to be articulated at home. In effect, the available familial reality of the household differed from its support group counterparts. Ethnographically, this offered a practical means of distinguishing organizations in their own right, not as formally or informally distinct social entities, but as descriptive domains. The upshot of this was that structures and their presenting organizations were heard in diverse folk interpretations and rhetoric as much as talk of things and events.

It bears repeating that an uncorrectable ethnographic lesson of the organizational embeddedness of social forms is that we should again write each form in hyphens. As far as experiential location is concerned, this would convey both the relational and the practical qualities of social objects. For example, Betty did not just have her family to think about, but the family-as-she-considered-it-at-home-at-times, in relation to other structurings and layers of hyphenated articulations. While the awkwardness of such a grammar attests to the ethnographic constraints of writing convention and graphic illustration, it does make a point about the nature of field reality—that field reality is simultaneously the practice of communication and a relationship between things and those concerned.

The Boundaries of Social Forms

Being both relationships and things, social forms are demarcated as much in, and about, organized social life, as they are distinct experiential objects. As such, the boundary of a social form is not just a property of the form as a thing (as we might think of a community perimeter) but a simultaneous limiting condition of its interpretive activity.

As the broken lines and overlapping area of Figure 4.2 suggest, the meaning of things and events is only *partially* bounded by the existing organized relevancies of the interpretive process. Partially is emphasized because the available structures in any organization are not isolated or fixed, but rather flow from one organization to another or are newly discovered in emergent interpretations. As such, the boundaries of social forms are tied to two types of organizational permeability. One is the result of the accumulation, combination, and interpenetration of organizational structures. This means that the available realities of, say, the family, are affected by conditions such as the range of professional familial orientations that permeate an organization. Each additional orientation provides yet another structure for interpreting domestic life. A second type of organizational permeability stems from the articulation process itself. Members continually ramify structures, and, thereby, social forms, by exemplifying out of individual experiences what things and events held in common could mean. I shall call the two, respectively, diffusive and articulative permeability, and illustrate them in turn. Together, they provide organizational cultures their dynamic horizons and serve to set and alter the boundaries of social forms.

Cedarview's official treatment language contained terms like tokens, costs, benefits, modification, programming, goals, baselines, post-baselines, targeting, and consequenting (Buckholdt and Gubrium, 1985 [1979]). The terms referenced what actually could be seen and heard in children's conduct, not what took place in the inner reaches of their minds. The language oriented more to the sum and substance of present and future behavior than to how the past informed the meaning of the present or forecast things to come. Behavioral principles informed what was called the GATG (Goal Attainment Treatment Guide), a documentary design for behavioral management by objective. As a private treatment vendor, the center contracted with county welfare departments to modify select inappropriate behaviors and to enhance appropriate ones in individually tailored programs. In turn, Cedarview was required to document programming and individual progress by means of the GATG.

In view of the official treatment orientation and language, children's experiences were candidates for individualization and quantitative assessment (see Gubrium, 1979). As far as individualization was concerned, while the school and the parents of a disturbed boy might complain of his constant teasing and bickering with his brothers and sisters at home, at Cedarview the boy's conduct officially and exclusively became his own, not his and his siblings'. It was then further individualized by the "targeting" of select portions for modification, for example, as "taunting behavior" or "swearing behavior." As such, within Cedarview's formal purview as a treatment facility, the boy was constructed into a case that virtually owned the conduct that ailed him. As far as assessment was concerned, it was the staff's responsibility to set specific numerical goals for targeted behaviors, for example, the goal that a boy or girl would tease half as much after six months of programming and treatment as initially. A program of rewards and punishments presented children with the benefits and costs of modifying or continuing targeted behaviors. Assessment further structured individual children's behaviors into baseline and postbaseline measures, providing a gauge of progress.

While, in written reports, children's conduct was officially communicated in behavioral language, it was evident that other languages and terms entered into the review process. Not all treatment staff had been professionally trained in behavior modification. In fact, one or two staff members were decidedly Rogerian, referring to Carl Rogers's person-centered approach to treatment. Some were more psychoanalytic, preferring to see children's conduct in terms of its past and deeper meaning, and taking what could be seen and heard in conduct as surface manifestations of essentially hidden structures. Cedarview's three psychological consultants were a behavioral psychologist, a Freudian psychiatrist, and a psychologist who took an eclectic view. The diverse demarcations of the normal and the pathological were additional categories for interpreting conduct, from the spirited sportsmanship considered earlier to the less benign classifications of emotional disturbance. Freudians did not always speak in their own terms, nor did behaviorists in theirs. In the course of articulating the children's behavior into meaningful categories, the social forms the behavior came to be ran a gamut of possible structurings. For example, discourses could form diverse personalities—a silly kid or an emotionally immature child, a deeply disturbed personality or an incorrigible individual, among others.

The structures and languages presented Cedarview staff with a considerable translation problem. I repeatedly heard staff members raise the question of "how to put" things and events in records and reports. The question was not peculiar to Cedarview, for it was regularly asked in each of the field sites studied in relation to the need to convey things and events diversely known in terms suitable for official internal or external consumption (see Gubrium, 1980).

The related paperwork, of which all staff members complained, was not just annoyance over the greater amount of time allocated to paper-and-pencil activity than to so-called one-on-one or hands-on care and treatment. It also reflected the often apparent differences in meaning suggested by alternate ways of putting things. For example, in a GATG training session, a special education teacher reported the tally of a child's fighting behaviors as five in a two-day period and then mentioned the difficulty presented by the possibility that it all "really" could be seen as one long fight, as the children involved contended. The teacher raised the issue of how to divide a child's visible activity into units when it was possible that the units were artificial facets of a uniform entity or a fight. The issue was a familiar one at Cedarview, the general question of how to translate between the behavioral arithmetic of tallies and counts, on the one hand, and the language of intention, on the other. Both were available means of structuring the children's experiences. Both made sense to those concerned, but it was also evident to some that the languages made different realities out of behavior. It was a different thing to report five fights in two days than one protracted fight. The translation problem was not just a matter of how to substitute one set of terms for another, but a matter of altering the very reality being represented. The issue was troublesome precisely because it was, simultaneously, a matter of both translation and transformation.

It was suggested to the teacher by a behavioral social worker attending the GATG training session that there would not be any problem if the teacher just recorded what she saw, not what she considered to be happening or what the children involved claimed. Ethnographically, I took the social worker's suggestion as a way of containing what was referred to earlier as diffusive permeability, a practical way of establishing the boundary of a social form. The form was inappropriate conduct; the issue was whether the child showed concrete quantitative evidence of being increasingly emotionally disturbed of late or on a comparative plateau. Interestingly, the teacher was grateful for the social worker's suggestion, thanked him, but added, "Ya know, the way I see it, it could still be one long fight." The comment, about what was real in the final analysis, was glossed over as the training session turned to other matters. Nonetheless, the exchange in general showed the work entailed in the articulation of structures and the practical considerations that enter into establishing the boundaries of things.

The before-and-after discourse of how-to-put-it questions showed evidence of how diffusive permeability figured in institutional accountability. While there were different structures available for assigning meaning to things in each organization, how-to-put-it questions designated official preferences. It was differences in these official preferences, perhaps more than any others, that distinguished one organization from another. Things and events could have many meanings in any of them; the how-to-put-it question signaled as much. But it also signaled an organization in name and purpose, formally distinguishing it as a particular domain of understanding.

Articulative permeability also affected the boundaries of social forms. I shall illustrate this by means of data gathered in the Alzheimer's disease support groups, although it was an interpretive condition common to all the field sites. Articulative permeability is culture making, in contrast to the diffusion of structures from one organization to another. While the support groups studied had a common public culture in that ideas and models of caregiving were shared along with the disease experience in general, each support group assigned what was shared to separate experiential particulars. In so doing, what was common became localized and created new interpretations.

Part of Alzheimer's disease's public culture are the caregiver celebrities whose stories appear throughout popular disease literature and media. The most celebrated victim of the disease is Rita Hayworth, the recently deceased Hollywood actress. Her disease story has appeared in mass circulation magazines like the *Ladies Home Journal* and has been cited repeatedly in others, along with such famous names as Edmund O'Brien and Norman Rockwell, who also died of Alzheimer's. Jerome Stone's story appears, too; he is the founder and current president of the Alzheimer's Disease and Related Disorders Association (ADRDA), whose wife has Alzheimer's. So do reports of the experience of Bobbie Glaze, whose care for a demented husband is widely known for its selfless devotion. Glaze also was active in founding and expanding the ADRDA chapter and support group network. There are more anonymous celebrities, too, like the five victims portrayed in the popular film *Someone I Once Knew,* which is frequently shown at chapter meetings and other local and national functions (see Gubrium, 1986).

Celebrated victims and caregivers can be thought of as exemplars of what the disease is like and how it is cared for. It was not uncommon in the support groups for questions to be asked about the cognitive or physical status of victims as well as the burdens of caregiving, and for responses to reference the exemplars. For example, when one asked what another's victim was like, the answer might be, "just like Priscilla in that movie we saw." Or it might be explained that a victim is not quite as bad as another well-known exemplar who had declined drastically. Even Alzheimer's itself, as a disease, was identified as what Rita Hayworth has, bringing immediate recognition. As exemplars, named and unnamed celebrities provided those concerned with a common ground for assigning meaning to their own and others' related experiences. The exemplars, in effect, were shared standards of comparison for deciphering personal experience.

Yet individual interpretations of the disease experience were not simply a matter of reproducing an existing public culture, but culturally productive in its own right. In one of the support groups studied, the adult children of Alzheimer's disease victims participated along with spouses of victims. One participant, Timothy, cared for a mother who had the disease. The mother lived in a small upstairs apartment in Timothy's home; he lived with his wife downstairs. Participants knew each other's circumstances, having heard about them many times. In this particular group, a few had been seriously considering the possibility of seeking nursing home placements for their victims. Timothy, for one, complained of the increasing strain his mother's decline was placing on his marriage.

Timothy's caregiving situation, his related sentiments, and future plans were sources of much discussion over the question of when "it's time" to seek institutionalization. Some sympathized with Timothy, stating that if things got as bad for them as Timothy reported they were for him, they, too, would consider a nursing home. Others felt that Timothy might be overreacting because, after all, there were any number of well-known cases of devoted home care for victims much worse than Timothy's mother. Timothy had described his mother as "just about getting to where that old, gray-haired woman is in that movie," referring to one of the five victims portrayed in the film *Someone I Once Knew*. Those disagreeing with Timothy used the same exemplar as a basis for arguing that perhaps Timothy's mother was not "that bad" yet because there were much worse cases being kept at home than the gray-haired woman. Ethnographically, one could literally hear participants using instances of a common culture to represent their own experiences. Agreed or disagreed, they recognized where they stood and formulated understandings of their individual responses to victims, both their own and Timothy's, in terms of what they shared. In turn, what they shared was assigned to Timothy's experience in different ways, making Timothy a devoted and long-suffering son for some and "too eager to dump his mother" for others.

Timothy's experience became part of the support group's folklore. Shortly after placing his mother into the nursing home that he had often described as one of the best in the region, Timothy left the support group—but his case didn't. Continuing participants frequently referred to Timothy and his mother in considering their own related experiences.

The things and events that Timothy had shared with them became, in their own rights, ways to structure what was now questioned and considered. When Theda, for example, remarked in distress that she just couldn't face the idea of placing her mother in a nursing home, she added, "like Timothy did." She cast further aspersion on Timothy's filial responsibility when she concluded, "and Mother's worse than she [Timothy's mother] was." Indeed, for a time, in this support group, Timothy was filial irresponsibility personified, a local sign of that particular family form. Participants used what they held in common with other support group members, as well as what they ostensibly came to realize in retrospect about Timothy, to draw connections between the desirable and undesirable in family life. In relation to a public culture, participants, in effect, made fine-grained structures out of bits and pieces of their own experiences that they, in turn, used to further articulate the caregiving experience and what it meant to "be family." As such, what they shared in common with others in the Alzheimer's disease experience and the public culture of the ADRDA returned to them in ever-changing forms and instances, permeating the known with the new.

5. CONCLUSION

Throughout our considerations, the concept of *field* has been left undefined. I used the term intuitively, in reference to the practical domain and engagement of the folk realities discussed. In this conclusion, I turn briefly to the field as a way of commenting on the nature of lived experience and folk realities. What those concerned put into effect, confront, or actually do in engaging structures and articulation informs us of the meaning of field and fieldwork.

The Field as Practice

To encounter the practice of folk interpretation is to come face to face with the voicing and voices of social structure. As noted earlier, neither we, as ethnographers, nor people in general, actually see or hear the social forms that Durkheim, for one, so forcefully persuaded us to treat as things. Yet Durkheim knew, too, that the forms are the realities that their respective fields of vision convey to us. People speak of this or that kind of family while pointing to members. They denote particular roles and select personalities as they gesture toward bodies and other voices, even their own. Their references and gestures convey two sides of the things and events that are more or less real to them: the latter's concrete everyday minutiae, which I have called things and events, and what the minutiae signal about the realities they represent.

The things and events of lived experience are material in that those concerned can literally point to them, as did Gary when he pointed to Tom's ladyfingers, or when a caregiver gestures toward a support group participant and indicates that the participant is a responsible and devoted wife. Yet we know, too, that as objects of people's references, the material is composed of things and events for those concerned. Separate from the latter, they are experientially nothing—no thing(s). What Gary, the caregiver, and others do in addressing material bits and pieces of everyday life is virtually to enliven them. A ladyfinger that signals connivance may draw a blow to Tom's ear; a ladyfinger conveying purveyance entices close inspection of what the firecrackers might bring—reasonable courses of action in their respective contexts. If they were not reasonable, we would expect to hear as much or indirectly infer the same, as folk do.

The material field that we, as ethnographers, address is practical, filled with both working actualities and potential realities, never just one or the other. As far as actualities are concerned, ladyfingers are not merely epiphenomenal traces of Tom's, Gary's, and Bill's more or less well-organized exchanges. What Tom, Gary, and Bill see right before their eyes is what holds their attention, not merely their concerted attention to the objects. Even while their attention occasionally becomes an object of interest in its own right, as they now argue or make comments about the respective bases of their assertions, no matter how multilayered their concern, it is still attentive, in the final analysis, to a presumed world of realities. As far as practice is concerned, we cannot faithfully read the meaning of firecrackers from conversational rules alone, nor from the analysis of folk philosophical categories. This is evident in the common caveats to "stick to business," "see for yourself," "get out of the clouds," "not just play games," "do what you have to," "get real," "be practical," and "know the ropes," among a host of telltale signs of engagement with a world of apparently concrete objects and events.

In regard to potential realities, we do an injustice to field practice when we take what people say to be "the way things (and events) are" at face value. Just as people know and say that "it's real out there," they understand, too, for better or worse, that the real is circumscribed by opinion, point of view, and a variety of conditions on which the real depends. It is the "it depends" quality of everyday life that suggests to us, as ethnographers, that the field is also a world of potential meanings.

Where do we place ourselves ethnographically in addressing a field of practice? What are we hearing and seeing as we listen to, and observe, folk in their everyday affairs? When we hear Tom speak of what he "can get for you," whose voice do we hear? As far as field practice is concerned, we simultaneously encounter Tom's voicing of what he is and what his purported action will mean, on the one side, and both implicit and emergent, yet shared, understandings of what Tom says could mean, on the other. We hear two voices in one, Tom's voicing of what the ladyfingers and his connection with them mean, together with a more or less discernible range of ways to structure his testimony. We know more about what Tom is saying and what happens in response to it than that of which Tom's and others' surface verbalizations inform us, just as those concerned do. I am not referring to motives, but to frames of reference or ways of structuring—attaching meaning to—whatever may be motivating the boys as well as the ostensible consequences of presumed motives. To understand is literally to stand under or away from what is going on, to consider what the latter could, or does, mean as a way of indicating as much.

Fieldwork

The field as practice is a field of signs, of things or events and what they represent. Because the meaning of things and events is a product of the interpretive work of those concerned, the field is always simultaneously a field of signalers, those engaged in the concrete business of everyday life. Accordingly, fieldwork is the activity of systematically documenting—making visible—the organization and transformation of fields of signs and signalers, what Tom's, Gary's, Bill's, and others' actions do and could mean, in and about the times and places their related affairs are engaged. This, of course, is another way of saying what we began with, namely, that field realities were a point of reference for seeing and conveying the folk philosophical details of people's lives, what literally makes their lives meaningful and what does not.

This brings us to the aim of fieldwork. While it might seem platitudinous to say so, fieldwork aims to be faithful to folk experience. We have argued that it is not enough simply to listen to people and heed their plain words, or to reconstruct the words' natural grammar, for what people themselves heed is not testimony alone, but what they take words to convey. For that reason, as fieldworkers, we must, to some degree, ignore what people actually say, just as they do, and attend to what they could be telling each other and us. Their conversations alone are inadequate to the task. They voice much more than they say. Indeed, they frequently tell us as much when they claim to know better than each other what their words mean. They even know that at certain times and in certain places, what is said and done "here" or "there" will mean one thing, not another.

While those concerned orient to matters underlying what they actually say, do, and denote, they know, too, that the route to the experiential logics of their lives runs through practice, not official charters per se, nor credentials, authority, or formal and informal activities as such. The latter avail them of structures of understanding, yes, but they are interpretive resources, not determinants. Of this, too, people tell us as they take charge over, or discharge, the representations they could, or believe they should, be to each other.

Fieldwork is not just a matter of carefully observing and systematically documenting what people say and do, not just a matter of the mechanics of recording speech and activity. That would not be faithful to folk experience. Rather, fieldwork involves participating with people in understanding everyday life, not vicariously, but analytically. It requires that we hear the philosophically astute voicing of the things and events of their worlds that simultaneously is heard by them and by us as voices other than their own. As Geertz (1983: 152) once put it, the "aim is to render obscure matters intelligible by providing them with an informing context." It requires, too, that we never lose sight of the practical work this entails. People tell us as much at particular times and places.

REFERENCES

Alzheimer's Disease and Related Disorders Association (1982) A Disease of the Century. Chicago: ADRDA.

ANDERSON, S. A. and D. A. BAGAROZZI (1983) "The use of family myths as an aid to strategic therapy." Journal of Family Therapy 5: 145-154.

BAGAROZZI, D. A. and S. ANDERSON (1982) "The evolution of family mythological systems: considerations for meaning, clinical assessment, and treatment." Journal of Psychoanalytic Anthropology 5: 71-90.

BARTOL, M. A. (1979) "Nonverbal communication in patients with Alzheimer's disease." Journal of Gerontological Nursing 5: 21-31.

BECKER, H. S. (1963) Outsiders. New York: Free Press.

BECKER, H. S. (1967) "Whose side are we on?" Social Problems 14: 239-247.

BERNARDES, J. (1984) "Do we really know what 'the family' is?" in P. Close and R. Collins (eds.) Family and Economy in Modern Society. London: Macmillan.

BERNARDES, J. (1985) "'Family ideology': identification and exploration." Sociological Review 33: 275-297.

BERNARDES, J. (forthcoming a) "Theorising 'family life,' I: 'doing things with words.'" Sociological Review: Sociology and Family Policy Debates.

BERNARDES, J. (forthcoming b) "Theorising 'family life,' II: founding the new 'family studies.'" Sociological Review: Sociology and Family Policy Debates.

BLAU, P. M. [ed.] (1975) Approaches to the Study of Social Structure. New York: Free Press.

BLUMER, H. (1969) Symbolic Interactionism. Englewood Cliffs, NJ: Prentice-Hall.

BOTT, E. (1957) Family and Social Network. New York: Free Press.

BUCKHOLDT, D. and J. F. GUBRIUM (1985 [1979]) Caretakers: Treating Emotionally Disturbed Children. Lanham, MD: University Press of America.

CARRITHERS, M., S. COLLINS, and S. LUKES (1985) The Category of the Person. New York: Cambridge University Press.

CICOUREL, A. V. (1972) "Basic and normative rules in the negotiation of status and role," in D. Sudnow (ed.) Studies in Social Interaction. New York: Free Press.

CICOUREL, A. V. and J. I. KITSUSE (1963) The Educational Decision Makers. Indianapolis: Bobbs-Merrill.

DENZIN, N. (1970a) The Research Act. Chicago: Aldine.

DENZIN, N. (1970b) "Symbolic interactionism and ethnomethodology," in J. D. Douglas (ed.) Understanding Everyday Life. Chicago: Aldine.

DERRIDA, J. (1973) Speech and Phenomena. Evanston, IL: Northwestern University Press.

DERRIDA, J. (1978) Writing and Difference. Chicago: University of Chicago Press.

DINGWALL, R. and P. M. STRONG (1985) "The interactional study of organizations: a critique and reformulation." Urban Life 14: 205-232.

76

DURKHEIM, E. (1961) The Elementary Forms of the Religious Life. New York: Collier-Macmillan.

DURKHEIM, E. (1964) The Rules of the Sociological Method. New York: Free Press.

FERREIRA, A. J. (1963) "Decision-making in normal and pathologic families." Archives of General Psychiatry 8: 68-73.

FOUCAULT, M. (1972 [1969]) The Archaeology of Knowledge (A. M. Sheridan Smith, trans.). New York: Random House.

FOUCAULT, M. (1981 [1977]) "Truth and power" (G. Gillan, trans.), in C. Lemert (ed.) French Sociology. New York: Columbia University Press.

FROST, P. J. et al. (1985) Organizational Culture. Newbury Park, CA: Sage.

GALLANT, M. J. and S. KLEINMAN (1983) "Symbolic interactionism vs. ethnomethodology." Symbolic Interaction 6: 1-18.

GALLANT, M. J. and S. KLEINMAN (1985) "Making sense of interpretations: response to Rawls on the debate between symbolic interactionism and ethnomethodology." Symbolic Interaction 8: 141-145.

GARFINKEL, H. (1967) Studies in Ethnomethodology. Englewood Cliffs, NJ: Prentice-Hall.

GEERTZ, C. (1973) The Interpretation of Cultures: Selected Essays. New York: Basic Books.

GEERTZ, C. (1983) Local Knowledge: Further Essays in Interpretive Anthropology. New York: Basic Books.

GIDDENS, A. (1979) Central Problems in Social Theory. Berkeley, CA: University of California Press.

GLASER, B. and A. STRAUSS (1968) Time for Dying. Chicago: Aldine.

GOFFMAN, E. (1959) The Presentation of Self in Everyday Life. New York: Doubleday Anchor.

GOFFMAN, E. (1961) "The moral career of the mental patient," in E. Goffman, Asylums. Garden City, NY: Doubleday Anchor.

GOFFMAN, E. (1974) Frame Analysis. New York: Harper & Row.

GUBRIUM, J. F. (1975) Living and Dying at Murray Manor. New York: St. Martin's.

GUBRIUM, J. F. (1979) "Observing the individual problems of human service records." Humanity & Society 4: 108-116.

GUBRIUM, J. F. (1980a) "Doing care plans in patient conferences." Social Science and Medicine 14A: 659-667.

GUBRIUM, J. F. (1980b) "Patient exclusion in geriatric staffings." Sociological Quarterly 21: 335-348.

GUBRIUM, J. F. (1986a) Oldtimers and Alzheimer's: The Descriptive Organization of Senility. Greenwich, CT: JAI Press.

GUBRIUM, J. F. (1986b) "The social preservation of mind: the Alzheimer's disease experience." Symbolic Interaction 9: 37-51.

GUBRIUM, J. F. (1987a) "Organizational embeddedness and family life," in Timothy Brubaker (ed.) Aging, Health & Family: Long-Term Care. Newbury Park, CA: Sage.

GUBRIUM, J. F. (1987b) "Structuring and destructuring the course of illness: the Alzheimer's disease experience." Sociology of Health and Illness 9: 1-24.

GUBRIUM, J. F. (forthcoming) "The family as project." Sociological Review.

GUBRIUM, J. F. and D. R. BUCKHOLDT (1977) Toward Maturity: The Social Processing of Human Development. San Francisco: Jossey-Bass.

GUBRIUM, J. F. and D. R. BUCKHOLDT (1982a) Describing Care: Image and Practice in Rehabilitation. Cambridge, MA: Oelgeschlager, Gunn & Hain.

GUBRIUM, J. F. and D. R. BUCKHOLDT (1982b) "Fictive family: everyday usage, analytic and human service considerations." American Anthropologist 84: 878-885.

GUBRIUM, J. F., D. R. BUCKHOLDT, and R. J. LYNOTT (1982) "Considerations on a theory of descriptive activity." Mid-American Review of Sociology 7: 17-35.

GUBRIUM, J. F. and J. A. HOLSTEIN (1987) "The private image: experiential location and method in family studies." Journal of Marriage and the Family 49: 773-786.

GUBRIUM, J. F. and R. J. LYNOTT (1985a) "Alzheimer's disease as biographical work," in W. A. Peterson and J. Quadagno (eds.) Social Bonds in Later Life. Newbury Park, CA: Sage.

GUBRIUM, J. F. and R. J. LYNOTT (1985b) "Family rhetoric as social order." Journal of Family Issues 6: 129-152.

HAMMERSLEY, M. and P. ATKINSON (1983) Ethnography: Principles in Practice. London: Tavistock.

HAYTER, J. (1974) "Patients who have Alzheimer's disease." American Journal of Nursing 74: 1460-1463.

HENRY, J. (1971) Pathways to Madness. New York: Random House.

HENRY, J. (1985 [1965]) "My life with the families of psychotic children," in G. Handel (ed.) The Psychosocial Interior of the Family. New York: Aldine.

HOLSTEIN, J. (1987) "Family rhetoric and involuntary mental hospitalization." Milwaukee, WI: Marquette University, Institute for Family Studies. (working paper)

JACKSON, D. D. (1973) "The question of family homeostasis." Psychiatric Quarterly 31: 79-90.

KURZWEIL, E. (1980) The Age of Structuralism. New York: Columbia University Press.

LAING, R. D. (1969) The Politics of the Family. New York: Random House.

LAING, R. D. and A. ESTERSON (1964) Sanity, Madness and the Family. Baltimore: Penguin.

LEMERT, C. C. (1979) Sociology and the Twilight of Man. Carbondale, IL: Southern Illinois University Press.

LYNOTT, R. J. (1983) "Alzheimer's disease and institutionalization: the ongoing construction of a decision." Journal of Family Issues 4: 559-574.

MACE, N. L. and P. V. RABINS (1981) The 36-Hour Day. Baltimore: Johns Hopkins University Press.

MEHAN, H. and H. WOOD (1975) The Reality of Ethnomethodology. New York: John Wiley.

MILLER, G. (1986) "Depicting family troubles: a micro-political analysis of the therapeutic interview." Journal of Strategic and Systemic Therapies 5: 1-13.

MILLER, G. (forthcoming) "Producing family problems: organization and uses of the family perspective and rhetoric in family therapy." Symbolic Interaction.

MILLS, C. W. (1959) The Sociological Imagination. New York: Oxford University Press.

MILLS, C. W. (1963) Power, Politics and People: The Collected Essays of C. Wright Mills (I. L. Horowitz, ed.). New York: Basic Books.

PERLMUTTER, M. and J. M. SAUER (forthcoming) "Induction, trance and ritual in family mythologizing." International Journal of Family Therapy.

POLLNER, M. (1978) "Constitutive and mundane versions of labeling theory." Human Studies 1: 269-288.

RAWLS, A. W. (1985) "Reply to Gallant and Kleinman on symbolic interactionism vs. ethnomethodology." Symbolic Interaction 8: 121-140.

REISBERG, B. (1981) Brain Failure. New York: Free Press.

RICOEUR, P. (1970) Freud and Philosophy: An Essay on Interpretation. New Haven: Yale University Press.

RYLE, G. (1949) The Concept of Mind. Chicago: University of Chicago Press.

SCHUTZ, A. (1963a) "Common sense and scientific interpretation of human action," in M. Natanson (ed.) Philosophy of the Social Sciences. New York: Random House.

SCHUTZ, A. (1963b) "Concept and theory formation in the social sciences," in M. Natanson (ed.) Philosophy of the Social Sciences. New York: Random House.

SCHUTZ, A. (1970) On Phenomenology and Social Relations (H. Wagner, ed.). Chicago: University of Chicago Press.

SILVERMAN, D. (1970) The Theory of Organizations. New York: Basic Books.

SILVERMAN, D. (1985) Qualitative Methodology and Sociology. Hampshire, England: Gower.

SNOW, C. P. (1959) The Two Cultures and the Scientific Revolution. New York: Cambridge University Press.

SUDNOW, D. [ed.] (1972) Studies in Social Interaction. New York: Free Press.

THOMAS, W. I. (1966) On Social Organization and Social Personality (M. Janowitz, ed.). Chicago: University of Chicago Press.

THORNE, B. and M. YALOM [eds.] (1982) Rethinking the Family. New York: Longmans.

TURNER, R. [ed.] (1974) Ethnomethodology. Baltimore: Penguin.

WARREN, C.A.B. and J. M. JOHNSON (1973) "A critique of labeling theory from the phenomenological perspective," in J. D. Douglas and R. Scott (eds.) Theoretical Perspectives on Deviance. New York: Basic Books.

WEBER, M. (1947) Theory of Social and Economic Organization. New York: Free Press.

WEBER, M. (1958) The Protestant Ethic and the Spirit of Capitalism. New York: Scribner.

WHYTE, W. F. (1955) Street Corner Society. Chicago: University of Chicago Press.

WIEDER, D. L. (1973) Language and Social Reality. The Hague: Mouton.

ZIMMERMAN, D. and D. L. WIEDER (1970) "Ethnomethodology and the problem of order: comment on Denzin," in J. D. Douglas (ed.) Understanding Everyday Life. Chicago: Aldine.

ABOUT THE AUTHOR

JABER GUBRIUM is Professor of Sociology at the University of Florida. He specializes in the interpretive analysis of aging and the life course. He has written extensively on the social organization of care in human service institutions. Among his books are *Living and Dying at Murray Manor* (1975) and *Oldtimers and Alzheimer's: The Descriptive Organization of Senility* (1986). Currently, he is developing a semiotic approach to the family as well as studying the narrative structure of longevity.

NOTES